THE
UNIX
PHILOSOPHY

THE
UNIX
PHILOSOPHY

Mike Gancarz

Digital Press
Boston • Oxford • Melbourne • Singapore • Toronto • Munich • New Delhi • Tokyo

Digital Press™ is an imprint of Butterworth–Heinemann, Publisher for Digital
Equipment Corporation.

UNIX is a registered trademark of UNIX System Laboratories, Inc., a wholly-owned
subsidiary of Novell, Inc.

All trademarks found herein are property of their respective owners.

Library of Congress Cataloging-in-Publication Data

Gancarz, Mike.
    The unix philosophy / by Mike Gancarz
        p.   cm.
    ISBN 1-55558-123-4
    1. UNIX (Computer file)   I. Title.
QA76.76.063G365   1995
005.4'3—dc20   94-25893
                                                                          CIP

For information, please contact:
Manager of Special Sales
Butterworth-Heinemann
225 Wildwood Avenue
Woburn, MA 01801-2041
Tel: 781-904-2500
Fax: 781-904-2620
For information on all Butterworth-Heinemann publications
available, contact our World Wide Web home page at:
http://www.bh.com

Transferred to digital printing 2006

Contents

v

8 ――――――――――――――――――――――――――

9 ――――――――――――――――――――――――――

Preface

I first became aware of the need for a book on the UNIX philosophy while teaching introductory UNIX courses to field service personnel in 1991 at Digital Equipment Corporation's Atlanta Customer Support Center. The technicians had been sent to me as interns, which was a polite way of saying that they could recite everything they knew about UNIX in about thirty seconds. They had a good grasp of hardware. However, hardware was rapidly becoming a commodity, turning them into "board swappers" on single-board systems. To retain their jobs, they suddenly found themselves crossing the abyss between hardware and software.

Throughout the lectures on basic UNIX usage, I watched the frustrated looks on the students' faces. Despite the detailed information they received about pipes, shells, and filters, they just weren't getting the message. They memorized how people did things with UNIX well enough, but they lacked understanding of "why UNIX?" in the first place.

This book offers an answer to that question. While most UNIX reference books today explain how to use UNIX and its amazing array of tools, *The UNIX Philosophy* examines the guiding principles behind it. It explores in new ways the reasons for small unifunctional programs, rapid prototyping, and portable software.

As a secondary goal, this book attempts to check the progress of look-alike systems that, while claiming to be UNIX, are moving away from the UNIX methodology. Brian W. Kernighan of UNIX System Laboratories recently expressed concern over the number of "crappy UNIXes" that had come along in recent years. I share his desire to keep the UNIX philosophy alive in those operating systems claiming to be UNIX.

WHO WILL BENEFIT FROM THIS BOOK

In the early days, only system programmers found UNIX material interesting. Today's UNIX users and developers comprise a diverse group with a variety of personal and professional interests. In this book I have tried to reach many of them by avoiding low-level technical details while providing thought-provoking views on the nature of UNIX.

The "fringe people" will find here an introduction to UNIX ideas without getting bogged down in command parameters, programmatic interfaces, and such. DP managers can learn enough about the UNIX approach to decide whether to commit resources to it. Skilled users of other operating systems who are moving to UNIX may discover ways to overcome their distrust of this seemingly radical operating system.

Novice UNIX users will benefit from learning the cornerstone ideas of UNIX contained here. The book will help them pass from rote memorization of UNIX commands to in-depth understanding of their underlying principles. I suggest that they read this book before plunging into the standard UNIX documentation or other reference books. Subsequent material will then make much more sense.

Experienced UNIX programmers should consider reading this book several times during their careers. Working in fast-paced, highly competitive engineering environments, there is great pressure to abscond with the principles of good software design under UNIX. Companies put great emphasis on using some development processes because they look good instead of ensuring that their approaches have sufficient substance. This book serves as a kind of sanity check when design issues appear impossible to resolve or solutions contain questionable assumptions.

Finally, people who deal with the abstract world of ideas will find value in learning about the UNIX philosophy. Many techniques used to develop software apply to other endeavors as well. Writers, graphic artists, teachers, and speakers may discover that rapid prototyping and leveraging work in their fields, too.

CHAPTER OVERVIEWS

Chapter 1—"The UNIX Philosophy: A Cast of Thousands" explores the history of the UNIX philosophy and how it came about. It also briefly describes the tenets of the UNIX philosophy as a prelude to the longer explanations provided in subsequent chapters.

Chapter 2—"One Small Step for Humankind" shows why small components are best for building large systems. It discusses their ability to interface well with each other, both in software systems and in the physical world. The last part of the chapter focuses on the importance of having programs that do one thing well.

Chapter 3—"Rapid Prototyping for Fun and Profit" stresses the necessity of constructing prototypes early when designing a successful product. A discussion of the Three Systems of Man illustrates the phases that all software passes through. It defends rapid prototyping as the fastest route to the Third System, the most correct of the three.

Chapter 4—"The Portability Priority" provides a different perspective on software portability. It emphasizes that software developers must choose between efficiency and portability in their designs. The Atari VCS is studied as a model of high efficiency and limited portability. The chapter also highlights data portability as an important, though often overlooked, goal. A case study of the typical UNIX user's collection of tools provides an excellent example of software longevity due to portability.

Chapter 5—"Now THAT'S Leverage" discusses the idea of "software leverage," where reusing components results in greater impact. We see how the use of shell scripts achieves a high degree of leverage.

Chapter 6—"The Perils of Interactive Programs" begins by defining Captive User Interfaces. It suggests that developers limit their usage and instead focus on making programs interact better with other programs. It expresses the idea that all programs are filters. The chapter ends with a discussion of filters in the UNIX environment.

Chapter 7—"More UNIX Philosophy: Ten Lesser Tenets" lists several notions that UNIX developers generally follow but don't consider primary elements of the UNIX philosophy. Since this chapter deals with some concepts at deeper levels than the rest of the book, the less technical reader should feel free to skip this chapter. UNIX purists, however, will likely find it quite entertaining.

Chapter 8—"Making UNIX Do One Thing Well" presents the UNIX mail handler MH as an example of how good UNIX applications are built. It finishes with a summary of the UNIX philosophy that shows how it derives its strength from each element working together.

Chapter 9—"UNIX and Other Operating System Philosophies" compares the UNIX philosophy to several other operating system philosophies to emphasize the uniqueness of the UNIX approach.

The text avoids many technical details as they vary from one UNIX implementation to another. Instead, it stresses that the UNIX philosophy is a design methodology that depends less on specifics and more on a general approach defined at a higher level.

I've tried to keep an upbeat tone throughout the book. While some people may enjoy reading massive technical tomes lacking humanity, the rest of us prefer writing that is both entertaining and informative, i.e., the "info-tainment" approach. This, too, is in keeping with the UNIX culture. The UNIX community has always had a wry sense of humor. It shows in places in the original UNIX documents and on the networks frequented by UNIX people. Perhaps it's why UNIX developers enjoy their work so much.

Do not be dissuaded by the levity, however. This is serious stuff. People have found or lost software fortunes by observing or ignoring the tenets covered here. Proper applications of the UNIX philosophy have usually resulted in tremendously successful products. Operating in direct conflict with these tenets has often caused developers to miss important windows of market opportunity.

Students of my lectures have mentioned that, while you may at first superficially absorb ideas expressed here, they return to your conscious mind at odd times. Powerful ideas tend to do that. If you have never been exposed to the UNIX philosophy before, prepare yourself for an interesting journey.

Acknowledgments

Even small books like this one can have a fair number of people whose contributions must be applauded. I am deeply grateful to the following individuals and organizations:

Mike Meehan, formerly of Digital Press, without whose vision of acquiring manuscripts for the UNIX market this book might never have gotten off the ground.

John Osborn and George Horesta, also formerly of Digital Press, who fanned the flames and kept the project on track, sometimes against all odds. (If you only knew!) I am also deeply indebted to John for offering his perspective on certain aspects which helped to clarify the book's intent.

Fred Avolio, Jon Hall, Donald Merusi, and Aaron Sawyer, who employed their broad knowledge of the UNIX operating system as technical reviewers of the manuscript and provided a hefty amount of moral support for a first-time author.

Brian Kernighan and Rob Pike, who made comments which convinced me that this book will serve a real need.

Pat Proctor, the best example of a Tupperware salesperson I've ever known.

xvi   *The UNIX Philosophy*

The software support specialists and interns at Digital's Atlanta Customer Support Center who helped me refine the presentation which later became the concept for the manuscript.

The Wordsmiths, a Christian Writers Group in Nashua, NH, for their encouragement in the latter stages of this project.

The folks at GeoWorks, whose *GeoWorks Ensemble 2.0* (a.k.a. "The Monster Upgrade") made the final stages of editing the manuscript much easier than it could have been.

Reference Software International, producers of *Grammatik V*, a tool which showed me at least 3,500 ways to improve my writing.

Adam and Sarah (a.k.a. "Rigor Mortis" and "Pandemonium"), who endured watching their Dad go off into the little room in the basement countless times to work on the first draft.

Vivian, the wind beneath my wings, who also provided useful commentary on selected portions of the book. Her patience endures forever.

MIKE GANCARZ
DIGITAL EQUIPMENT CORPORATION
NASHUA, NEW HAMPSHIRE

Introduction

An operating system is a living, breathing software entity. The soul of the computing machine, it is the nervous system that turns electrons and silicon into a personality. It brings life to the computer.

An operating system, by its nature, embodies the philosophy of its creators. The Apple Mac/OS, with its highly visual, object-oriented user interface, proclaims "it's right there in front of you." Microsoft's MS-DOS, the undisputed leader of the personal computer revolution, tries to bring "a taste of the mainframe" to the desktop. Digital Equipment Corporation's OpenVMS assumes that the user fears the electronic thinking machine and must be given only a few powerful choices to accomplish a task.

The creators of the UNIX operating system started with a radical concept: They assumed that the users of their software would be computer literate from the start. The entire UNIX philosophy revolves around the idea that the user knows what he is doing. While other operating system designers take great pains to accommodate the breadth of users from novice to expert, the designers of UNIX took an inhospitable "if you can't understand it, you don't belong here" kind of approach.

It was precisely this attitude that prevented UNIX from gaining wide acceptance early. It was confined to the back room where academics studied it because of the intoxicating fumes it brought to the ivory towers ("The parallels one can draw between the UNIX file system hierarchy and the natural order of things bears careful intellectual scrutiny") and "techies" tinkered with it because it gave them more ways to play than any other system before it.

Alas, the commercial world could see no value in it. It was a hacker's toy, a curiosity. Few profitable enterprises would dare risk their investment returns on an operating system that came from a research lab, was nurtured in universities, and was self-supported by the purchaser. As a result, UNIX languished for more than 15 years as an unsung hero.

Then an amazing thing happened in the early 1980's. Rumors began to circulate that there was an operating system that provided more flexibility, more portability, and more capability than whatever it was that people were currently using. Furthermore, it was universally available at very little cost and it could run on just about anyone's machine.

The message of UNIX sounded nearly too good to be true, but history has a way of proving that we often shoot the messenger. Whenever any radical idea comes along that seriously alters our view of the world, our natural tendency is to bash the bearer of new tidings. As far as anyone in the computing mainstream could see, these "UNIX fanatics" were not interested in evolution—they were talking revolution.

As UNIX began to infiltrate the computing world, evidently many in today's corporate bureaucracies abhorred the thought of revolution. They preferred their ordered world on PC's and mainframes, secure in the belief that job security came from knowing the simple commands that they'd struggled to learn and use in their daily tasks. UNIX became The Enemy, not so much because it was intrinsically evil, but because it threatened the status quo.

For years UNIX pioneers lived in relative obscurity. Support for their radical ideas was nowhere to be found. Even when some sympathetic soul would listen to the tirades of the local UNIX advocate, the response would usually be "UNIX is okay, but if you want to do anything serious, you should probably use _____." (Fill the blank with the name of your favorite mainstream operating system.) Still, operating system philosophies are like religions. When someone has it in their head that they have found The Truth, they're not willing to let it go that easily. So the UNIX apostles pressed on, doggedly upholding the standard, believing that someday the world would be converted and they would see software paradise.

While the commercial world was busy building barriers to UNIX, the academic world was welcoming UNIX with open arms. A generation of young people raised in houses with color TV's, microwave ovens, and video games was entering universities that had obtained UNIX for the cost of the magnetic media on which it was distributed. These young people had clean canvases for minds and the professors were more than willing to paint on them a picture of computing far removed from the mainstream.

The rest is history.

Today UNIX is rapidly gaining acceptance in situations where it once would have been considered unthinkable. It is the undisputed system of choice in the academic world, and its applications in the military and commercial worlds are expanding daily.

I have been telling people for years that it is only a matter of time before UNIX becomes the world's operating system. I have yet to be proven wrong. Ironically, however, the world's operating system will not be called "UNIX," for as companies have realized the value of the name, their lawyers have rushed to register its trademark. As a result, interfaces will be designed, standards will be proposed, and many applications will be written in the name of "open systems." Rest assured, though, that the UNIX philosophy will be the driving force behind them all.

The UNIX Philosophy:
A Cast of Thousands

1

The philosophy of one century is the common sense of the next.
—CHINESE FORTUNE COOKIE

Many people credit Ken Thompson of AT&T with inventing the UNIX operating system and, in a sense, they're right. Thompson wrote the first UNIX version in 1969 at AT&T's Research Division of Bell Laboratories in Murray Hill, New Jersey. It ran on a Digital PDP-7 minicomputer as a platform for the program Space Travel. Space Travel originally ran on the Multics system, developed at the Massachusetts Institute of Technology.

UNIX is based on Multics, one of the first timesharing operating systems. Before the development of Multics, most computer operating systems operated in batch mode, forcing programmers to edit large stacks of punched cards or paper tape. Programming in those days was a very time-consuming process. It was a period when the saying "Heaven help the twit who drops his box of punch cards" was readily understood by all.

Thompson borrowed many features of Multics and included them in his early versions of UNIX, the principal characteristic being that of timesharing. Without this capability, most of the features taken for granted in today's UNIX systems—and in most other operating systems for that matter—would lack real power.

By borrowing ideas from Multics, Thompson embarked upon a course of action that has become a well-worn path (no pun intended) for UNIX developers: good programmers write great software; great programmers "steal" great software. No, we're not implying that Thompson was a thief. But his willingness to avoid the NIH (not invented here) syndrome in some respects and yet add creative value in others helped launch possibly the most ingenious operating system in history. We'll explore the significance of "stealing" software later. For now, bear in mind that an idea shared is worth two kept in the brain.

People marvel at the portability of UNIX, but it wasn't always portable. Thompson originally coded it in assembly language. In 1972 he rewrote it in a portable language called B. Another member of AT&T's staff at Bell Laboratories, Dennis Ritchie, made extensive modifications to B in 1973, evolving it into the C language loved and despised today by programmers the world over.

Again, Thompson had set a precedent that was later adopted by UNIX developers: great programs are often written by someone whose back is against the wall. When an application must be written and (a) it must be done to meet a practical need, (b) there aren't any "experts" around who would know how to write it, and (c) there is no time to do it "right," the odds are very good that an outstanding piece of software will be written. In Thompson's case, he needed an operating system written in a portable language because he had to move his programs from one hardware architecture to another. No self-described portable operating system experts could be found. And he certainly didn't have time to do it "right."

Ken Thompson played a limited role in the development of the overall UNIX philosophy, however. Although he made significant design contributions in the areas of file system structure, pipes, the I/O subsystem, and portability, much of the UNIX philosophy came about as a result of many peoples' efforts. Each person who worked with UNIX in its early days helped give it shape in their area of expertise. The following table lists some contributors and their primary contributions.

Alfred Aho	Pattern scanning, parsing, sorting
Eric Allman	Electronic mail
Kenneth Arnold	Screen updating
Stephen Bourne	Command language
Lorinda Cherry	Interactive calculator
Steven Feldman	Computer-aided software engineering
Stephen Johnson	Compiler design tools
William Joy	Text editing, C-like command language
Brian Kernighan	Regular expressions, programming principles, typesetting, computer-aided instruction
Michael Lesk	High-level text formatting, dial-up networking
John Mashey	Command interpreter
Robert Morris	Desk calculator
D. A. Nowitz	Dial-up networking
Joseph Ossanna	Text formatting language
Dennis Ritchie	C programming language
Larry Wall	Patch utility, Perl command language, *rn* network news reader
Peter Weinberger	Pattern scanning

Although the above individuals are the earliest and most visible participants in the UNIX phenomenon, the people who developed the UNIX approach to computing eventually numbered in the thousands. Virtually every published paper on a major UNIX component lists more than a handful of contributors who helped make it happen. These contributors formed the UNIX philosophy as it is understood and propagated today.

THE UNIX PHILOSOPHY IN A NUTSHELL

The tenets of the UNIX philosophy are deceptively simple. They are so simple, in fact, that people tend to regard them as having little importance. That's where the deception comes in. Their simplicity disguises the fact that these ideas are incredibly effective when carried out consistently.

The following list will give you an idea of *what* the UNIX philosophy tenets are. The rest of the book will help you to understand *why* they are important.

1. *Small is beautiful.* Small things have tremendous advantages over their larger counterparts. Among these is the ability to combine with other small things in unique and useful ways.
2. *Make each program do one thing well.* By focusing on a single task, a program can eliminate much extraneous code that often results in excess overhead, unnecessary complexity, and a lack of flexibility.
3. *Build a prototype as soon as possible.* Most people would agree that prototyping is a valuable element of any project. But whereas prototyping is only a small part of the design phase under other methodologies, under UNIX it is the principal vehicle for generating an effective design.
4. *Choose portability over efficiency.* When UNIX broke new ground as the first portable operating system of any significance, it was big news. Today portability is taken for granted as a necessity in any modern software design, an example of a tenet that has gained wide acceptance on other systems besides UNIX.
5. *Store numerical data in flat ASCII files.* The choice between portability and efficiency addresses the value of portable

code. Portable data is at least as important as—if not more important than—portable code. Portable data is the often-neglected part of the portability formula.

6. *Use software leverage to your advantage.* Many programmers have only a superficial understanding of the importance of reusable code modules. Code re-use helps one take advantage of software leverage, a powerful concept that some UNIX developers use to create numerous applications in comparatively short time.

7. *Use shell scripts to increase leverage and portability.* Shell scripts are a double-edged sword for enhancing both software leverage and portability in a design. Whenever possible, writing a script instead of a complete C program is the way to go.

8. *Avoid captive user interfaces.* Some commands have user interfaces known to UNIX developers as "captive" user interfaces. These prevent the user from running other commands while the command is in use, effectively making the user a captive to the system for the duration of the command. Hence the name captive user interface.

9. *Make every program a filter.* The fundamental nature of all software programs is that they only modify data, not create it. Therefore, they should be written to perform as filters since they *are* filters.

The preceding list contains tenets about which UNIX developers are dogmatic. You will find similar lists in other books on UNIX, as they are the points that everyone considers to be foundational concepts of UNIX. If you adopt them, you will be considered to be a "UNIX person."

The following list contains ten lesser tenets, ideas which tend to be part of the UNIX world's belief system. Not everyone involved with UNIX is dogmatic about these, and some of them aren't strictly characteristic of UNIX. Still, they seem to be a part of the UNIX culture.

1. *Allow the user to tailor the environment.* UNIX users like the ability to control their environment—all of it. Many UNIX applications decidedly refrain from making decisions about styles of interaction and instead leave the choices to the user.

2. *Make operating system kernels small and lightweight.* Despite the never-ending push for new features, UNIX developers prefer to keep the most central part of an operating system small. They don't always succeed at this, but this is their goal.

3. *Use lower case and keep it short.* Using lower case characters is a tradition in the UNIX environment that has persisted long after the reason for doing so disappeared. Many UNIX users today use lower case commands and cryptic names because they want to, not because they're forced to anymore.

4. *Save trees.* UNIX users generally frown on using paper listings. There are good reasons for keeping all text online and using powerful tools to manipulate it.

5. *Silence is golden.* UNIX commands are notoriously silent when it comes to producing detailed error messages. Although more experienced UNIX users consider this a desirable trait, many users of other operating systems would beg to differ.

6. *Think parallel.* Most tasks can be broken down into a series of smaller subtasks. These subtasks can then be run in parallel to accomplish more in the same amount of time as one large task. A significant amount of activity occurs around symmetric multiprocessing (SMP) designs today, an example of a general trend in the computer industry towards parallelization.

7. *The sum of the parts is greater than the whole.* This tenet stems from the idea that a large application built from a collection of smaller programs is more flexible and hence more useful than a single large program. The same functional capability may exist in both solutions, but

the collection-of-small-programs approach is the more forward-looking of the two.

8. *Look for the 90 percent solution.* Doing 100 percent of anything is difficult. Doing only 90 percent is far more efficient and cost effective. UNIX developers often look for solutions that satisfy 90 percent of the target user base, leaving the other 10 percent to fend for itself.

9. *Worse is better.* UNIX aficionados believe that a "least common denominator" system is the one most likely to survive. That which is cheap but effective is far more likely to proliferate than that which is high quality and expensive. The PC-compatible world borrowed this idea from the UNIX world and is making quite a go of it.

10. *Think hierarchically.* UNIX users and developers prefer to organize things hierarchically. For example, the UNIX directory structure was among the first tree-structured architectures applied to file systems. UNIX has extended hierarchical thinking to other areas, such as network service naming, window management, and object-oriented development.

After reading the list of tenets, you may be wondering just what all the fuss is about. "Small is beautiful" is not such a big deal. "Do one thing well" sounds pretty narrow-minded in and of itself. Choosing portability over efficiency isn't the sort of idea that will change the world.

Is that all there is to UNIX?

Perhaps we should mention that Volkswagen built a marketing campaign around "small is beautiful" that helped them sell *millions* of automobiles. Or consider that Sun Microsystems, a leading UNIX systems vendor, based its strategy on "all the wood behind one arrowhead" or, in other words, "do one thing well." Could the growing interest in mobile computing have something to with *portability*?

Come. Let us begin the journey.

2

One Small Step for Humankind

About twenty years ago, when Americans drove big cars and were the envy of citizens in other countries, Volkswagen ran an ad campaign with the theme "small is beautiful." At the time it seemed like the German automobile manufacturer was out of touch with reality. Their VW Bug, while enormously successful in Europe, looked a little silly on the American landscape, like a midget in a land of giants. Still, Volkswagen kept driving home their message that small cars were here to stay.

Then the unforeseen occurred: Middle Eastern oil ministers showed the world that, yes, indeed, they could agree on something, namely a much higher price on a barrel of oil. By stubbornly withholding enormous quantities of crude, they tilted the supply and demand equation in favor of the suppliers. The price of gasoline rose well over one dollar a gallon. Gas lines appeared everywhere as the oil ministers held the world by its jugular vein.

Americans, long known for their love affair with big cars, began to discover that small truly *was* beautiful. They demanded smaller cars from the auto manufacturers to salve their aching wallets, and VW was there to oblige. What was once a "funny little car" now became a chic necessity.

Over time, people found that small cars enjoyed certain advantages over their larger counterparts. Besides relishing the increased gas mileage, they liked the way a small car handled—more like a British sports car than an ocean liner on wheels. Squeezing them into tight parking spots was a breeze. Their simplicity made them easy to maintain.

About the same time that the American affinity for small cars blossomed, a group of researchers in AT&T Bell Labs in New Jersey found that small software programs enjoyed certain advantages, too. They learned that small programs, like small cars, handled better, were more adaptable, and were easier to maintain than large programs.

This brings us to the first tenet of the UNIX philosophy:

TENET 1
Small Is Beautiful

If you're going to write a program, start small and keep it small. Whether you're crafting a simple filter tool, a graphics package, or a gargantuan database, work to reduce it to the tiniest piece of software practicable. Resist the temptation to turn it into a monolith. Strive for simplicity.

Traditional programmers often harbor a secret desire to write the Great American Program. When they embark on a development project, it seems like they want to spend weeks, months, or even years trying to solve the entire world's problems with one program. Not only is this costly from a business standpoint, it ignores reality. In the real world, few problems exist that cannot be surmounted using small solutions. We choose to implement such massive solutions because we don't fully understand the problem.

The science fiction writer Theodore Sturgeon once wrote that "90% of science fiction is crud. But then 90% of everything is crud." The same applies to most traditional software. A large portion of the code in any program is devoted to something other than actually performing its stated task.

Skeptical? Let's look at an example. Suppose you wanted to write a program to copy file A to file B. These are some steps that a typical file copy program might perform.

1. Query the user for the name of the source file.
2. Check whether the source file exists.
3. If the source file doesn't exist, notify the user.
4. Query the user for the name of the destination file.
5. Check whether the destination file exists.
6. If the destination file exists, ask the user if he wants to replace it.
7. Open the source file.
8. Inform the user if the source file is empty. If so, exit.
9. Open the destination file.
10. Copy the data from the source file to the destination file.
11. Close the source file.
12. Close the destination file.

Note that step ten does the file copy. The other steps perform functions that, although necessary, have little to do with copying the file. Under closer scrutiny, you'll find that the other steps can generally be applied to many other tasks besides file copying. They happen to be used here, but they're not really part of the task.

A good UNIX program should provide capabilities similar to step ten and little else. Carrying this notion further, a program strictly following the UNIX philosophy would expect to be given valid source and destination file names at invocation. It would have the sole responsibility of copying the data. Obviously, if all the program had to do was copy the data, it would be a very small program indeed.

This still leaves us with the question of where the valid source and destination file names come from. The answer is simple: from other small programs. These other programs perform the functions of obtaining a file name, checking whether the file exists, and determining whether it contains more than zero bytes of data.

"Now wait a minute," you may be thinking. Are we saying that UNIX contains programs that merely check whether a file exists? In a word, yes. The standard UNIX distribution comes with hundreds of small commands and utility programs that by themselves do little. Some, such as the *test* command, do apparently mundane functions like determining a file's readability or whether two strings passed as command line parameters are equivalent. If that doesn't sound very important, realize that the *test* command is one of the most heavily used UNIX commands.

By themselves, small programs don't do very much. They often perform one or two functions and little else. Combine them, however, and you begin to experience real power. The whole becomes greater than the sum of the parts. Large, complex tasks can be handled with ease. You can write new applications by simply entering them on the command line.

SOFTWARE ENGINEERING MADE EASY

It has often been said that UNIX offers the world's richest environment for programmers. One reason is that tasks that can be difficult, if not impossible, to accomplish on other operating systems are comparatively easy to accomplish under UNIX. Could it be that small programs make such tasks easy? Absolutely.

Small programs are easy to understand

Their "all business" approach keeps fluff to a minimum, focusing instead on performing one function well. They contain only a few algorithms, most of which directly relate to the job involved.

Large programs, on the other hand, lean toward complexity and present barriers to understanding. The bigger a program becomes, the more it gets away from its author. The sheer number of code lines begins to be overwhelming. For example, the programmer may forget which files the program's subroutines are found in or have trouble cross-referencing variables and remembering their usage. Debugging the code becomes a nightmarish task.

Some programs can be difficult to understand, whatever their size, simply because the nature of the function they do is inherently obscure. Such programs are rare, however. Most small programs are readily understood even by programmers with moderate experience. This is a distinct advantage of small programs over their larger counterparts.

At this juncture, you may be wondering at what point a small program becomes a large program. The answer is, it depends. Large programs in one environment may be considered average for another. What is spaghetti code to one programmer may be daily pasta to the next. Here are some signs that suggest that your software may be departing from the UNIX approach.

- The number of parameters passed to a function call causes the line length on the screen to be exceeded.
- Subroutine code exceeds the length of the screen or a standard piece of 8½-by-11 inch paper. Note that smaller fonts and taller windows on a large workstation monitor allow you to comfortably stretch the limit a bit. Just don't get carried away.
- You can no longer remember what a subroutine does without having to read the comments in the code.
- The names of modules scroll off the screen when you do an *ls* command. (*Ls* is the UNIX equivalent of *dir* on other operating systems.)
- You discover that one file has become too unwieldy for defining the program's global variables.
- You're still developing the program, and you cannot remember what condition causes a given error message.
- You find yourself having to print the source code on paper to help you organize it better.

These warning signs are likely to ruffle the feathers of some programmers, namely those in the "big is better" camp. Not every program can be made small, they say. This world is a pretty big place, and there are some pretty big problems out there that we're trying to solve with some pretty big computers. These problems require that we write some pretty big programs.

That's a pretty big misconception.

There exists a kind of software engineer who takes pride in writing large programs that are impossible for anyone but himself to comprehend. He considers such work "job security." You might say that the only thing bigger than his ego is his last application program. Such software engineers are far too common in traditional software engineering environments.

The problem with this approach to job security is that the companies they work for inevitably realize that eventually the person will move on, and they will be left holding the bag. The wiser companies take steps to prevent that. They hire individuals who understand that easily maintained software is more valuable.

No longer can the software designer say, "Heaven help the next guy." Good designers must go out of their way to make their software easy to maintain. They comment their code thoroughly—but not too thoroughly. They keep subroutines short. They pare the code down to what is absolutely necessary. The result usually is small programs that are easier to maintain.

Small programs are easy to maintain

Since a small program is usually easy to understand, it is likely to be easy to maintain as well, for understanding a program is the first step in maintaining it. No doubt you've heard this before, but many programmers ignore the subject of maintenance. They figure that if they took the time to write a program, then someone else will be just as willing to take the time to maintain it after them.

Most software engineers are not satisfied with maintaining other peoples' programs for a living. They believe—perhaps rightfully so—that the real money is made in writing new programs, not fixing past mistakes. Unfortunately, users don't see it quite the same way. They expect software to work the first time. If it doesn't, they get very upset with the program's vendor. Companies that fail to maintain their software do not remain in business for long.

Since maintaining software is not very glamorous work, programmers seek out ways to make the task easier or even avoid it altogether. Most cannot eliminate this duty entirely, however. If they're lucky, they probably could turn over maintenance chores to a junior individual. But more often than not, software support responsibilities usually fall upon the original author. So he must settle for making the task more palatable any way he can. Small programs meet this need quite nicely.

Small programs consume fewer system resources

Because their executable images occupy very little memory, the operating system finds it much easier to allocate space for them. This greatly reduces the need for swapping and paging, often resulting in significant performance gains. A popular term in the UNIX world is "lightweight," i.e., small programs often are considered lightweight processes.

Large programs, with their huge binary images, extract a heavy price from the operating system when loaded. Paging and swapping commonly occur, causing performance to suffer. Operating system designers, aware of the resource requirements of large programs, attempt to deal with this issue by building enhancements such as dynamic loading and sharable runtime libraries. These address the symptom, not the problem.

A computer hardware engineer I met in the early days of my career often joked, "All programmers ever want is MORE CORE! All we need to stop your whining is to give you another memory board." He was partly right, of course. Give a programmer more memory, and the programs will run faster and take less time to write, greatly increasing productivity.

Reflect upon the "more core" cure for a moment. My hardware engineer friend unwittingly based his statements on the tendency of the programmers in his sphere to write large, complex programs. It's not surprising. The operating system we were using for applications development then was not UNIX.

Had we been using UNIX and embracing its small program philosophy, the need for more memory would have been less evident. Then the joke would have been, "All programmers ever want is MORE MIPS!" (MIPS stands for "Millions of Instructions Per Second," a popular though not necessarily accurate measure of CPU performance.)

Why has the metric of MIPS become such a hot issue in the computer world today? Because as UNIX usage has become more prevalent, the use of small programs has proliferated as well. Small programs, although usurping little system memory when executing, derive the most benefit from the injection of additional CPU horsepower. Load them into memory, do their job quickly, and free up the memory for use by other small programs. Obviously, if the CPU capacity is lacking, then each program must spend a longer time in memory before the next small program can be loaded to do its job.

Systems employing small programs benefit from additional memory, however. Larger amounts of memory allow more small programs to run concurrently without relying on secondary storage. As we shall see later, the more small programs you can run at once, the higher the performance. This forms the basis of one tenet of the UNIX philosophy that we'll be discussing later.

Another area in which small programs have an edge in resource consumption has to do with the amount of disk space occupied by the programs themselves. Small programs, since they are performing a limited task, tend to require smaller executable images. The average small program takes up far less disk space than the typical large, monolithic program. Savings of 500K or more don't sound like much in these days of cheap CD-ROM prices, but when you're dealing with a system containing hundreds of programs, the differences can really add up.

The X Window System from the Massachusetts Institute of Technology is an excellent example of the dangers of large programs. Early versions of the X Window System were lean and mean. They ran quite comfortably on a system having as little as four megabytes of main memory. (Although four megabytes may not sound like a lot in today's PC world, X crammed an incredible array of features and portability into those four megabytes.)

The applications that ran on these early versions of the X Window System were also lean and mean. Although they lacked much of the sex appeal of today's user interfaces, they ran very fast on machines in the 1-MIPS range. Their impressive customization features made them state-of-the-art when they were released. They broke much new ground in the area of client-server display models. They did all of this using very few system resources.

Then along came X11. Designed by a committee of nearly thirty experts—the first warning sign—it is loaded with hundreds of new features. A window system for all reasons, it takes the notion of "user customizability" to its ultimate conclusion, i.e., the user can customize everything to his own liking without having to recompile the program's source code. Because of this incredible adaptability, users adopted it as the de facto window system of the UNIX world.

Unfortunately, X11 is no longer a small program. Typical applications under X11 require one megabyte of disk space or more for the user interface libraries alone. Nearly everything runs much more slowly than on earlier versions. Applications development using its various "standard tool kits" is downright painful. Even worse, while early X Window System implementations needed as few as four megabytes of main memory, many vendors today recommend a whopping sixteen megabytes of RAM for a basic system.

The same hardware engineer who poked fun at the software engineer's desire for more core was also fond of another saying: no matter how fast they can make the hardware run, software engineers will always find a way to slow it down for the user. As long as programmers continue to write large, monolithic programs like X11, he will be right.

Small programs are easier to combine with other tools

Anyone who has ever worked with large, complex programs knows this. Monolithic programs are worlds unto themselves. In trying to provide every feature that anyone could possibly want in a single program, they build barriers that hinder easy interfacing with other applications.

What about a large application that offers many conversions to other data formats? Isn't it really more valuable than a small program that allows only one data format? On the surface, that sounds like a plausible assumption. As long as the format needed happens to be one that the application already supports, you'll get along just fine. But what happens when the application must interface with a data format that it wasn't equipped to handle?

Software developers generally write large programs under the mistaken notion that they have dealt with all contingencies, i.e., their program can interface with whatever data formats exist today. This can be a problem. Although the developers can deal with today's data formats, they have no idea what new formats may come along that would render their application obsolete. The writer of a large, complex program operates under the egotistical assumption that the future is not only predictable, it's not going to differ much from today.

Authors of small programs, on the other hand, implicitly avoid foretelling the future. The only assumption they make about tomorrow is that it will be different from today. New interfaces appear. Data formats evolve. Styles of interaction rise or fall from the public favor. New hardware renders old algorithms obsolete. Change is inevitable.

In summary, you enjoy distinct advantages by writing small programs instead of large ones. Their simplicity makes them easier to write, understand, and maintain. You will find that both people and machines find them more accommodating. Most important, you will equip your programs to deal with situations you couldn't possibly have anticipated when you wrote them.

Look to the future. It will be here sooner than you think.

Let's take a moment to talk about a bug. Not a software bug. The other kind of bug.

A peculiar species of flying insect inhabits the area around Lake Victoria, a source of the Nile River. Spectacular video footage by explorer Jacques Cousteau shows this insect, known as a lake fly, congregating in thick, foglike masses on the lake and in a nearby jungle. Similar to mosquitoes in size and appearance, they sometimes form clouds over the lake so dense that one could easily mistake them for waterspouts or small tornadoes.

Large flocks of birds often swoop down into these "bug-spouts" to feast on nature's sufficiency, consuming millions of insects in a single air raid. Despite the predatory onslaught, though, millions more insects persist, their shadowy swarms exhibiting few signs of attrition.

When he more closely examined the life cycle of these unusual insects, Cousteau discovered that the adult lives for an exceedingly short period—about six to twelve hours. Even if they don't wind up as lunch for one of our feathered friends, their adult existence consists of little more than a brief flutter in the sunlight.

Just what does an insect that spends its entire adult life stage in a single day do with all that time? It attempts to propagate the species. It tries to squeeze what we human beings spend years doing into a few hours. Evidently it succeeds, for the species continues and in respectable numbers. If survival of the species is their goal, then these tiny winged nothings have set their priorities straight.

These flies have but one thing to do in life, and they do it well. UNIX developers believe that software should do the same.

TENET 2
Make Each Program Do One Thing Well

The best program, like Cousteau's lake fly, does but one task in its life and does it well. The program is loaded into memory, accomplishes its function, and then gets out of the way to allow the next single-minded program to begin. This sounds simple, yet it may surprise you how many software developers have difficulty sticking to this singular goal.

Software engineers often fall prey to "creeping featurism," as it's called in the industry. A programmer may write a simple application, only to find his creative urges taking over, causing him to add a feature here or an option there. Soon he has a veritable hodgepodge of capabilities, many of which add little value beyond the original intent of the program. Some of these inventions may have merit. (We're not talking about stifling creativity here!) But the writer must consider whether they belong in this chunk of code. The following group of questions would be a good starting point.

- Does the program require user interaction? Could the user supply the necessary parameters in a file or on the command line?
- Does the program require input data to be formatted in a special way? Are there other programs on the system that could do the formatting?
- Does the program require the output data to be formatted in a special way? Is plain ASCII text sufficient?
- Does another program exist that does a similar function without your having to write a new program?

The answer to the first three questions is usually no. Applications that truly demand direct user interaction are rare. Most programs get along fine without having to incorporate dialogue parsers in their routines. Similarly, most programs can satisfy most needs by using standard input and output data formats. For those cases where a special format is desired, a different general-purpose program can be used to make the conversion. Otherwise, each new program must reinvent the wheel, so to speak.

The UNIX *ls* command is an excellent example of a UNIX application gone astray. At last count, it had more than twenty options, with no end in sight. It seems as if the number of options grows with each new version of UNIX. Rather than pick on an esoteric feature, however, let's look at one of its more basic functions, specifically, the way it formats its output. *Ls* in its purest form should list the names of the files in a directory (in no particular order) like this:

```
/usr/home/gancarz-> ls
txt
doc
scripts
bin
calendar
X11
database
people
Mail
slides
projects
personal
bitmaps
src
memos
```

However, most versions of *ls* format output like this:

```
Mail        calendar    people      slides
X11         database    personal    src
bin         doc         projects    txt
bitmaps     memos       scripts
```

Listing the files in neat columns seems like a sensible thing to do . . . at first. But now *ls* contains code that does column formatting, a task that has little to do with listing the contents of a directory. Column formatting can be simple or complex, depending on the environment in which it is used. For example, *ls* assumes that the terminal will be eighty characters wide. What happens to the columns when invoking *ls* on, say, a window system where the terminal window is 132 characters wide? Suppose the user would prefer to view the output in two columns instead of four? What if the terminal uses a variable-width character set? Suppose the user would prefer to follow every fifth line of file names with a solid line? The list goes on.

In all fairness, *ls* retains the ability to list the contents of a directory one file per line. That is about all it should do, and leave the column work to other commands better suited to formatting tasks. *Ls* would then be a much smaller command, i.e., easier to understand, easier to maintain, using fewer system resources, and so on.

Since writing an application that does one thing well results in a smaller program, the two tenets complement each other. Small programs tend to be unifunctional. Unifunctional programs tend to be small.

A hidden benefit of this approach is that you remain focused on the current task, distilling it to the essence of what you're trying to accomplish. If you cannot make the program do one thing well, then you probably don't comprehend the problem you're trying to solve. In a later chapter, we'll discuss how to acquire that understanding the UNIX way. For now, think small. Do one thing well.

If a lake fly on the Nile River can do it, how hard can it be?

Rapid Prototyping
for Fun and Profit

The Ramans do everything in threes.

—ARTHUR C. CLARKE, *Rendezvous with Rama*

If you'll take a random walk down Wall Street, you'll soon discover that the average amateur investor doesn't know what he's doing. To make money in the stock market, everyone knows you must buy low and sell high. Yet year after year, the wolves fleece the lambs out of millions of dollars. It's well documented that the "little guys"—meaning you and me—are mostly wrong most of the time.

Many institutional investors don't do much better either. Most pension fund managers, mutual fund portfolio managers, and professional money managers have displayed an uncanny inability to beat the market consistently year after year, though many command annual salaries over a million dollars.

Recent studies have shown that index funds, which invest in securities represented by an index such as the Standard & Poor's

500, have outperformed 77 percent of all mutual funds on a long term basis. Despite the hype in the financial world about hot investment opportunities, the published records elucidate a stark reality: most of us can do about as well as any other investor, amateur or professional, by throwing darts at the stock pages of the newspaper and buying the stocks found thereunder.

Although it is extremely difficult to beat the market consistently, some do. Peter Lynch, renowned former manager of the Fidelity Magellan Fund, racked up an impressive record in the 1980s, making his clients very wealthy. Warren Buffett, the "Oracle of Omaha," has reaped enormous profits for stockholders in Berkshire Hathaway. Sir John Templeton has made similar fortunes by seeking investment bargains the world over.

Despite their successes, these legendary investors readily admit that they don't always get it right. They tell stories of the companies in which they had complete confidence whose stocks lost over half of their value in the year they purchased them. They lament the "ones that got away," the unlikely stocks that went on to score in the 1,000 percent range and higher. Though their performance far exceeds the norm in the investments, they know that they still have a lot to learn.

Other professionals have a lot to learn, too. Doctors must constantly strive to remain abreast of recent medical research developments. Accountants must learn new changes in the tax laws. Lawyers must study recent court decisions. Actuaries, salespersons, truck drivers, assemblers, plumbers, electricians, judges, researchers, dog catchers, engineers—they all have something to learn.

The fact is, everyone is on a learning curve

Think about it. When was the last time you met someone who knew the exact result of an action every time without fail? I'm not saying that such people don't exist. I'm only suggesting that they are rare. Such ability usually requires plenty of hard work and study plus a dose of good luck.

Engineers offer perhaps the best living proof that most people are still learning. For example, if aeronautical engineers know everything there is to know about aeronautics, then why do they need test pilots? Why do General Motors' engineers road test their cars? Why do computer engineers subject their products to a field test before putting them into mass production? If engineers had complete knowledge of what they were doing, quality assurance departments would be unnecessary because the quality would be built into the products during the developmental phase.

Software engineers are particularly burdened with a steep learning curve. Software is elusively difficult to write correctly the first time. The software engineering profession consists of constant revision, a job where trial and error are the norm and applications are born out of countless hours of frustrating rework.

Note that we're not saying that people cannot master anything. It's just that it takes longer than most people suspect. The average learning curve extends further and inclines more steeply than it first appears. So many variables exist in the world today that mastery can consume a lifetime, and complete knowledge may not even be attainable at all.

Even the masters know that changes are inevitable

It's a rare project indeed that doesn't require changes to the original specifications. Marketing requirements shift. Suppliers fail to deliver. Critical components may perform differently than specified. Prototypes and test runs expose design flaws. These factors make producing sophisticated technology the most delicate of tasks.

Faulty communication frequently bears the responsibility for changes. When a product's prospective end user tries to explain his needs, many gaps exist in the description. He may omit something or perhaps fail to convey with sufficient accuracy the details of what he has in mind. So the engineer uses his imagination to fill the gaps. He takes the description, looks it over, and begins to apply his own biases to the design. Sometimes the engineer tries to second-guess the end user or assumes "he really wants it this way, not that." Even worse, the engineer is often separated from the end user by corporate individuals such as product managers, the sales team, and support personnel who add further distortion to the end user's desired outcome.

We see through a glass darkly. Beyond the smoke and mirrors, reality dictates that we will not get it right the first time. It's better to face this axiom first. Changing a product early in the product cycle costs far less than undertaking major revisions later.

Why do you think they call it "software"?

Software engineering requires more rework and encompassing of modifications than any other engineering discipline. This is because software deals with abstract ideas. If people have difficulty describing hardware accurately enough to get it right the first time, imagine how difficult it is to describe something that exists only in peoples' minds and in electrical patterns traversing a microchip. The admonishment, "Abandon all hope, all ye who enter here" comes to mind.

If end users could specify precisely what they wanted—if software engineers had complete knowledge of users' needs today and what they will need in the future—then we would not need software. Every program written would be placed in ROM the first time around. Unfortunately, such a perfect world doesn't exist.

In my early days as a software engineer, I used to strive for software perfection. I would write and rewrite subroutines until they were as fast and clean as they could be. I reviewed code repeatedly, hoping to make it even marginally better. I added new features (creeping featurism, really) as the ideas for them came along. I blissfully carried out this charade until my boss snapped me back to reality.

"It's time to ship it," he declared.

"B-but it's not done yet! Just give me a couple more days to—"

"Software is never finished. It is only released."

Once a piece of software is released, no one really knows what will happen to it. Experienced engineers may have a vague notion of the consumer's demographics, the kind of environment it will be used in, and so on. But they would be hard pressed to reliably predict the eventual success or failure of any software product.

The UNIX developers certainly didn't know what would happen to UNIX. Nor did the developers of MS-DOS, OpenVMS, and every other operating system for that matter. Every new O/S takes its designers into uncharted waters. Their only hope consists of continually gathering progress reports and then correcting the course accordingly.

For example, did Ken Thompson realize the importance of portability when he wrote the first UNIX kernel? Evidently not, for he wrote early UNIX kernels in assembly language. He rewrote them later in a higher-level language, altering his original direction. Did Dennis Ritchie anticipate that C would become a universal programming language, one voted on in standards committees? Hardly. His reissue of his classic *The C Programming Language* contained modifications to the language specification that affirmed that he didn't get it right the first time either.

So most of us are still learning. Even if we're egotistical enough to think that we know it all, someone will change the requirements on us. How then are we to build software? The next tenet holds the key.

TENET 3
Build a Prototype As Soon As Possible

When we say "as soon as possible," we mean AS SOON AS POSSIBLE. Post haste. Spend a small amount of time planning the application, and then GET TO IT. Write code as if your life depended on it. Strike while the terminal is warm. You haven't a nanosecond to waste!

This idea runs counter to what many would consider "proper engineering methodology." Most have been told that you should fully design an application before embarking on the coding phase. "You must write a functional specification," they say. "Hold regular reviews to ensure that you're on track. Write a design specification to clarify your thoughts on the details. 90 percent of the design should be done before you ever fire up the compiler."

These guidelines sound fine in principle, but they fail to place enough emphasis on the prototype. It is in the building of the prototype that the idea is first tested for merit in a visual, realistic way. Before then, you have little more than a collection of thoughts about the way something ought to work. The concept is barely understood at that point, and it is highly unlikely that everyone perceives it in the same way. You need a consensus of perception before the project can proceed. The prototype moves toward that consensus by providing a concrete representation of the goal.

Prototyping is a learning process

The sooner it begins, the closer you will be to the released product. The prototype shows you what works and—most importantly—what doesn't. You need this affirmation or denial of the path you've chosen. It is far better to discover a faulty assumption early and suffer only a minor setback than to spend months in development meetings unaware of the Mother of All Design Problems waiting to ambush you three weeks before the deadline.

Early prototyping reduces risk

You have something concrete that you can point to and say "It's going to look like this." If you can show it to trusted users to get their reactions, you may learn that your design was on target. More often than not, your prototype will come back shot full of holes. That's okay, though. You have gained valuable design information. It is better to weather the ripples of a small group of critics than to watch a million potential users turn their backs on your product.

For every correct design, there are hundreds of incorrect ones. By knocking out a few of the bad ones early, you begin a process of elimination that invariably brings you closer to a quality finished product. You discover algorithms that do not compute, timings that keep missing a beat, and user interfaces that cannot interface. These trials serve to winnow out the chaff, leaving you with solid grain.

Most people agree that prototyping has many advantages. Even the academics who teach more traditional software engineering methodologies readily recognize its value. However, prototyping is a means to an end, not the end in itself. The goal of all prototyping should be to build something we call the Third System. Before we can talk about the Third System, though, we need to talk about the other two systems that came before it.

THE THREE SYSTEMS OF MAN

Man has the capacity to build only three systems. No matter how hard he may try, no matter how many hours, months, or years he may struggle, he eventually realizes that he is incapable of anything more. He simply cannot build a fourth. To believe otherwise is self-delusion.

Why only three? That is a tough question. One could speculate on several theories drawn from scientific, philosophical, and religious viewpoints. Each could offer a plausible explanation for why this occurs. But the simplest explanation may be that the design process of man's systems, like man himself, passes through three stages of life: youth, maturity, and old age.

In the youthful stage, people are full of vigor. The new kids on the block, they exude vitality, crave for attention, and show lots of potential. As a person passes from youth to maturity, he or she becomes more "useful" to the world. Careers take shape. Longer term relationships develop. Influence widens in worldly affairs. The person makes an impact—good, bad, or otherwise. By the time old age sets in, the person has lost many abilities of youth. As physical prowess declines, much of the person's worldly influence fades as well. One's career becomes a memory. Resistance to change sets in. What remains is valuable wisdom based on experience.

Man's systems pass through these same stages in their development. Each system possesses characteristics that correlate to corresponding periods in life. All systems follow a path beginning at youth, transiting into maturity, and ending in old age.

Just as some men and women never reach old age, so some systems fail to mature as well. Often this is due to external circumstances. Development plans may change. Funding for a project may be withdrawn. A potential customer may change his mind and decide to shop somewhere else. Any number of these factors could serve to prevent the system from reaching maturity. Under normal conditions, though, man carries the systems through all three stages. For our purposes we refer to these stages as the Three Systems of Man.

Most UNIX developers don't know the Three Systems of Man by name, but they readily attest that they exist. Let's take a closer look at some of their characteristics.

THE FIRST SYSTEM OF MAN

Man builds the First System with his back against the wall

Usually he is under pressure to meet a deadline or satisfy other time-critical demands. This ignites a creative spark within him. Eventually the spark becomes a small flame as he spends hours in intense deliberation, turning the idea over repeatedly in his mind. Work continues. His creative instincts begin to really take hold. The flame grows brighter.

At some point he becomes aware of aspects of his idea that go beyond simply reaching his goal. He feels as though he has stumbled upon something far more important. The goal fades somewhat, but not before he has convinced himself that his idea provides the solution.

He has no time to do it "right"

If he had the time to do it "right," he wouldn't be under any deadline pressure. So he has to improvise. But whereas the typical improvisation is one of compromise, this effort roars ahead without compromise—in the wrong direction. At least, that is what his observers conclude. When a person's back is against the wall without time to do it "right," he tends to break all the rules. He appears to traditional-thinking coworkers as if he has "lost his marbles under the refrigerator."

Criticism often rises against him. "He can't get away with that!" they insist. "He doesn't know what he's doing. He's going about it all wrong." His response? "Yeah, it's ugly, but it works!"

The lack of time to do it right forces him to focus on the important aspects of the task and to ignore the nonessentials. As a result, he plans to leave some details to later versions. Note that he may never complete any later versions. The belief that he will "fill in the blanks" in the future, however, serves to dissuade him from becoming sidetracked and also provides an excuse for any shortcomings in the first version.

Man builds the First System alone or, at most, with a small group of people

This is partly because many people in the mainstream have little appreciation for what he's doing. They have not seen what he has seen from his vantage point, so they have no idea why he's excited. Hence, they conclude that his work is interesting but not interesting enough for them to get involved.

A second reason that many people tend to avoid working on the First System is a more practical one: risk. Building the First System involves significant risk. No one knows if the First System will have the characteristics that lead to the development of the Second System. There always exists a better than 80 percent chance of failure. Being associated with a First System that failed can be "career limiting," in industry jargon. Consequently, some people would rather wait until the idea is proven. (They usually become the developers of the Second System. More about them later.)

When a small group builds the First System, it does so with high motivation. Things happen quickly. A kind of synergy infuses the team, resulting in a strong, cohesive unit sharing a common vision and having an intense desire to bring the system to fruition. They understand the goal and toil feverishly to reach it. Working with such a group can be at once exhilarating and exhausting, not to mention very rewarding if the system succeeds.

One thing is certain: the First System is almost never built by a large group of people. Once the team grows too big for daily personal interaction among its members, productivity wanes. Personalities clash. People carry out hidden agendas. Little fiefdoms emerge as people begin to pursue their selfish interests. These activities dilute the goal, making it difficult to reach.

Fred Brooks, in his book *The Mythical Man-Month*, points out that adding more programmers to a development project too late in the effort makes it later, not earlier. UNIX people have known this for years.

The First System is a "lean, mean, computing machine"

It achieves high performance at minimal cost. Its developers had to take the expedient approach in most areas, forcing them to "hard-wire" much of the application code. Such software trades features and flexibility for simplicity and speed. Frills are saved for the next version. Anything orthogonal to the system's goal is left out. The software gets the job done—and little else.

People generally marvel at the First System's performance when they compare it to a more mature system that they're familiar with. They wonder why their system cannot compete with the new kid on the disk block. They bemoan the fact that this little upstart outperforms their favorite on the popular benchmarks. It doesn't seem fair, and it isn't. Comparing a First System to a system in its *n*th release is inviting an apples-to-oranges comparison. The designers had different goals in mind.

The First System displays a concept that ignites others' imaginations

It causes people to engage in wild flights of fancy of the "what if...?" variety. It whets their appetite for more: more features, more functionality, more everything. People say things like "Think of the possibilities!" and "Imagine what we could do with this at Gamma BioTech!"

The following lists some ideas and technologies where innovation is setting peoples' imaginations on fire, spawning many First Systems today:

Artificial intelligence

Biotechnology

CD-ROM

Content-based text retrieval

Digital imaging

Digitized sound

Electronic monetary systems

Genetic engineering

Information superhighway

Interactive television

Mobile computing

Multimedia applications

Quality (Six Sigma, Total Quality Management, etc.)

Unified world government

Virtual reality

The concept that ignites other peoples' imaginations becomes the chief reason the Second System follows the first. If there is nothing exciting going on with the First System, then everyone concludes that it meets their needs and (yawn!) they have something better to do. Many a First System has died in its infancy because it failed to inspire its observers to do great and wonderful things with it.

THE SECOND SYSTEM OF MAN

The Second System is a strange beast. Of the three systems that man builds, it garners the most attention, often going on to become a commercial success. Depending on the size of its market, it may capture the hearts and minds of thousands or even millions of users. Yet, ironically, in many ways the Second System is the worst of the three.

"Experts" build the Second System using ideas proven in the First System

Attracted by the First System's early success, they climb aboard for the ride, hoping to reap rewards by having their name attached to the system. Everyone wants to be associated with a winner.

This group of self-proclaimed experts often contains many critics of the First System. These individuals, feeling angry with themselves for not having designed the First System, lash out at its originators, spewing forth claims that they could have done it better. Sometimes they are right. They could have done a better job on certain aspects of the design. Their specialized knowledge can prove very helpful in redesigning several more primitive algorithms found in the First System. Remember: The First System's designer(s) had little time to do it "right." Many of these experts know what is "right" and have the time to carry it out.

On the other hand, some of these experts are trying to dump a load of sour grapes on someone's hard-won success. Usually this smacks of NIH, the ever-popular not invented here syndrome. Although many of these individuals could produce the First System, they were beaten to the punch. Rather than join the fun, they hope to receive credit for "having improved the obviously amateurish attempts of the original designers" by seeking to replace the First System's mechanisms with their own.

Such attitudes often invoke the ire of the First System's designers. Occasionally they fight back. Bob Scheifler, a pioneer of the popular X Window System, once responded to critics of his early design efforts in handy fashion: "If you don't like it, you're free to write your own industry-standard window system."

The Second System is designed by a committee

Whereas the First System is typically the brainchild of less than seven people, possibly thirty people or more contribute to the Second System's design. The First System's success acts like a magnet. It draws in many people who may have even a remote interest in its thought-provoking ideas. Some of these people have a sincere desire to further the earlier designers' ideas; others just want to go along for the ride.

The Second System's design committee carries out its business very publicly. It posts meetings announcements in highly visible network repositories, user group newsletters, and other well-known information channels. It publishes design documents that proudly display the names of all contributors. The committee tries to ensure that all participants get credit where credit is due . . . and occasionally even where it's not due. If a committee builds a sidewalk, its members all want to write their initials in the cement.

In spite of (as opposed to because of) the activities that occur, some real design work takes place. A few committee members sign up to produce key design pieces and may deliver quality software. Others play "devil's advocate" roles in helping the committee render an honest solution. Still others offer launch points for interesting discussions that ultimately serve to clarify the new design.

Unfortunately, the design-by-committee approach involves drawbacks. It is nearly impossible for a group (an organizational body having at least two individuals) to agree on all salient points. For participants to feel valued, each must believe he or she has contributed something to the general design, no matter whether they have any expertise in the design area. It doesn't matter whether they are right or wrong. They argue for the sake of their own justification, for the chance to say to themselves "I can hold my own with these experts and therefore that makes me an expert, too." When you add up all the design contributions, though, you wind up with an elephant when what you really wanted was a gazelle.

The Second System is fat and slow

It possesses opposite characteristics of the First System, i.e. where the First System was lean and mean, the Second System lumbers along like an enormous giant. If the First System required a minimum of one megabyte of memory, then the Second System refuses to run in anything less than four. People praised the First System for its high throughput on a one MIPS machine; users bemoan the Second System's "turtle" performance on a ten MIPS machine.

"It's because the Second System has more features," says the committee. "You get what you pay for."

The Second System *does* have more features. Its impressive array of capabilities accounts for part of its success, but the average user takes advantage of only a fraction of these. The rest just get in the way. As a result, the Second System runs slower because it must deal with its copious "advantages."

Often the only way to make it run faster is to buy more hardware. I've long held a belief that computer manufacturers love the Second System for this reason. In these days of portable software, most Second Systems will run on nearly any vendor's platform, provided it is big enough. To take advantage of the new technology, however, customers often must invest in new equipment. The massive size of the Second System virtually guarantees huge numbers of product sales: faster CPU's, larger disks, higher-capacity tape drives, and plenty of memory chips. This spells big profits for hardware vendors.

So the Second System is a mixed blessing. You get lots of features, some of which you might even use. And you get the chance to convince your boss that it's time to buy a new machine.

The world hails the Second System as a great achievement with much pomp and circumstance

It makes a big splash in the marketplace. It garners instant commercial acclaim for its "flexibility, wide range of options, and expandability." Vendors praise its virtues: it delivers tomorrow's technology today. It goes far beyond existing systems in every respect. It's the last system you'll ever need.

The Herd, overwhelmed by this hype, looks to the Experts for answers. The Experts willingly accommodate them. Any member of the design committee (which by now has grown to several hundred members) instantly gains respect as an Expert. Others climb the ladder of credibility by critiquing the work of the design committee.

Interest in the system grows. It becomes the media's darling. Magazines spring up to track its progress. Books appear to explain its mysteries. Conferences are held for the serious minded to discuss its future. Seminars help the less enlightened explore its past. The phenomenon builds momentum as more followers join the ranks of the informed and the initiated.

Once the Herd is convinced by all the hype that the Second System is an outstanding system, it remains stubbornly so. For example, the X Window System incorporates many features beyond its basic windowing capabilities. Most of these are seldom used, and their presence drastically impairs general performance. Still, X survives because it is a Second System. Despite its shortcomings, it has enough momentum to overcome any other window system in the UNIX marketplace. It reigns supreme. As a Second System, no other system could take its place.

Except the Third System.

THE THIRD SYSTEM OF MAN

The Third System is built by people who have been "burned" by the Second System

After several months or several years, some people begin discovering that the Second System isn't all that it was cracked up to be. They have learned that it runs slowly as it devours system resources. It was designed by experts, some of whom were experts by self-proclamation only. In trying to meet everyone's needs, the Second System has met no one's needs in any complete sense.

Soon the Second System has burned many people. They have learned that the "last system you'll ever need" is merely one of many such systems. Too many user groups have been formed. Seminars are now taught by people on the fringes of the activity sphere. These individuals are not as sharp as the ones who'd fed the fever earlier, so the quality level goes way down. Oceans of rhetoric fill the user conferences as peripheral individuals, having seen the Experts become famous, hope to emulate their panache. They're too late.

Eventually the whisper that the Second System is less than perfect turns into an outcry of disgruntled users. Everyone becomes convinced that there has to be a better way. At that point, the world is ripe for the Third System.

The Third System is born out of rebellion against the Second System.

The Third System usually involves a major name change from the Second System

By the time the Third System arrives, the First System's originators have disappeared. The most innovative people involved in the Second System's development have moved on to more interesting projects as well. No one wants to be associated with a future trailing-edge technology.

While the transition from the first to the second rides on soaring wings of new hope, the transition from the second to the third is like a ride on the Titanic: Everyone heads for the lifeboats as it becomes obvious that metal doesn't float.

The X Window System again provides us with a real-world example. X10 was the first implementation that became available as a commercial product from a major vendor. Its characteristics were typically found in a First System: high performance, few frills, and an exciting concept. When X11 came along, it fulfilled the essence of the Second System in every respect and developed a wide following. Eventually a Third System will replace X11. It will not be called "X12," however. By then X will be regarded as an obsolete implementation of a commonplace technology.

The original concept is still intact and is regarded as obvious

Recalling the First System, you remember that it displayed a concept that set peoples' imaginations on fire. By the time the Third System appears, the concept will be understood and accepted by all. Everyone who uses the system acknowledges that "that's the way it should be done." The idea responsible for the First and Second Systems' development still exists in the Third System. It was tried in the fire and found true.

Examples abound of original concepts once regarded as innovative that are commonplace today. Consider ink. Once upon a time, people used a feather with ink to write on parchment paper. Eventually, the fountain pen replaced the feather. In recent years (comparatively speaking), ballpoint pens have become the standard writing tools in everyday usage. In the future, you're likely to see new writing tools that make today's ballpoint pens seem archaic. Don't be surprised, though, to find that they still use ink. The use of a liquid medium to transfer our thoughts to paper is an original idea that has survived several different containers. As long as we have paper, we will have ink.

The Third System combines the best characteristics of the First and Second systems

The First System had very high performance but lacked some necessary features. In the Second System, the pendulum swung back in the direction of more features at the expense of poor performance. In the Third System the perfect balance is struck. Only the features truly needed remain. As a result, the system requires a modest amount of resources and accomplishes much with them.

Another factor in the Third System's high performance is the contributions of experts—not the "pseudo-experts" spoken of earlier but sincere, motivated individuals who possess real talent and make effective contributions to the system's evolution. Their efforts enhance the system in specific, meaningful ways. Their work, like the original enlightening idea, stands the test of time.

Efforts to place the software in ROM have likely been unsuccessful in the first two systems due to the changing nature of software. One should never put "opinion" in ROM. By the time the Third System comes along, however, designers have a solid understanding of what works and what doesn't. Things have gelled to the point where putting the software into hardware then becomes a real possibility.

Finally, the Third System's designers are usually given the time to do it "right"

The size of the task is well understood and the risks are small because they are working with a proven technology. Decision makers can create accurate budgets and schedules for its implementation.

BUILDING THE THIRD SYSTEM

The goal then is to build the Third System, for it is that which gives everyone the biggest return for the effort expended. Containing the perfect mix of features, resource consumption, and performance, it includes only those features that people actually use. It strikes a proper balance between the amount of disk space, memory, and CPU cycles used versus the level of performance delivered. Users recommend it, and customers buy it year in and year out.

How do you build the Third System? You build the other two systems first. There is no other way. Any attempt to change the order merely guarantees that you will build more First or Second Systems than would otherwise be necessary.

There are some shortcuts, though. The secret is to progress from the First to the Third System as quickly as possible. The more time spent on building the first two systems, the longer it will take to achieve the Third System's optimum balance. If you keep the cycles involved in building the First and Second Systems short and iterative, you will arrive at the Third System faster.

Although producing the Third System is the goal of both UNIX developers and those following "traditional" software engineering methodologies alike, the UNIX developers take a radical approach. First, consider the way most software is written:

1. Think about the system design.
2. Build a prototype to test your assumptions.
3. Write detailed functional and design specifications.
4. Write the code.
5. Test the software.
6. Fix bugs and design flaws found during the field test, updating the specifications as you go.

The traditional software engineering methodology was invented by those who believe that it is possible to get it right the first time. "If you're going to build a system," they say, "you may as well build the Third System." The problem is, no one knows what the Third System is until it's built.

The traditionalists like to see everything written down, as if having written specifications to the *n*th detail assures them that they have considered all design factors. The notion that "90 percent of the design should be complete before you write the first line of code," comes from the belief that excellent designs require forethought. They believe that by fully documenting the design, you guarantee that you have investigated all viable possibilities, and by having complete specifications, you keep things organized and ultimately increase your efficiency.

The traditional methodology results in very good specifications early and poor specifications later. As the project gets underway, schedule pressures force the engineers to spend progressively more time on the software and less time on the specifications. Such a shift in priorities causes the specs to become out of sync with the actual product. Given a choice between a product with little documentation versus ample design specifications without a product, software developers always choose the former. People will not pay them for specifications without a product behind them.

UNIX developers take an alternate view toward detailed functional and design specifications. Although their intent is similar to that of the traditionalists, the order of events differs:

1. Write a short functional specification.
2. Write the software.
3. Use an iterative test/rewrite process until you get it right.
4. Write detailed documentation, if necessary.

A "short" functional specification here usually means three to four pages or less. The rationale behind this is that: (a) no one really knows what is wanted at first, and (b) it's hard to write about something that doesn't exist. While a traditionalist may spend weeks or even months writing functional and design specifications, the UNIX programmer jots down what is known about the goal at the start and spends the rest of the time building the system.

How does the UNIX programmer know if he's proceeding in the right direction? He doesn't. Neither does the traditionalist. Eventually the design must be shown to the prospective end user. The difference is, the traditionalist presents to the user a massive tome containing a boring description of what the system is going to be like. The UNIX programmer shows the user a functional application.

The traditionalist wonders whether the final product will meet his needs. He cannot be sure that he communicated his requirements effectively, nor can he be certain that the implementation will match the specifications.

On the other hand, the UNIX approach provides the user with a functional First System that he can see and touch. He begins to get a feel for how the final product will operate. If he likes what he sees, fine. If not, it's far easier to make major changes now instead of later.

Remember, though, that a characteristic of the First System is that it displays a concept that ignites others' imaginations. Viewing a "live" implementation of the First System sets off a creative spark in the user's mind. He starts to imagine what he might do with the product. This spark feeds on itself, and he begins to think of new uses, some of which may not have been thought of by the original designers.

At this point the UNIX approach leapfrogs over the traditional engineering method. While the traditionalist's user wonders how the product will look, the UNIX developer's user is already thinking of what to do with the working prototype.

For the UNIX user, the iterative design process has begun. He and the developers are proceeding toward the Third System. Once the developers receive the initial reactions from the users, they know if they are on the right track. Occasionally the user may inform them that what he wanted is not what he received, resulting in a complete redesign. More often than not, the user will like part of the design and will provide useful commentary on what must be changed. Such cooperation between the developers and the end user is tantamount to producing a Third System that meets the user's needs in most respects.

The best time to write a detailed design specification is after the iterative design process is complete. Of course, by then a lengthy spec may not be necessary, since it is mainly intended for the developers and interested third parties to read and review. The users and the developers have been reviewing the application throughout the iterative design process, so writing a detailed spec at this point may not serve any useful purpose. If one is still required for some reason, it is far easier to document an existing application.

Some people have expressed concern that the UNIX approach to software development, although quite suitable for small systems, does not work for larger ones. They argue that beginning the coding phase without a thorough design is engineering suicide. They claim that lack of adequate forethought can only lead to disaster.

We're not saying that one should plunge into coding a large system without an adequate design, however. Some amount of deliberation is necessary in order to define proper goals. It's just not very useful to document every detail before proceeding because the details are likely to change.

Also consider that while UNIX has had the benefit of very little up-front design, it has evolved into a system capable of handling tasks once relegated to larger systems. A system of its stature traditionally would have required countless tomes of functional specifications and detailed design documents. Plenty of UNIX documentation exists today through the efforts of a few enterprising technical publishers, but most of it describes designs that already exist. Original specifications are practically nonexistent.

Unlike most systems planned in the traditional way, UNIX evolved from a prototype. It grew out of a series of design iterations that have transformed it from a limited-use laboratory system into one called upon to tackle the most ardent tasks. It is living proof of a design philosophy that, although unorthodox to some, produces excellent results.

4

The Portability Priority

So there I was, an attendee at the 1991 Summer USENIX Technical Conference, strolling the halls of Nashville's Opryland Hotel, reveling in the grandiose luxury of that country music citadel, picking my way through the crowds, hoping to happen upon someone famous, and basking in the satisfaction of having just signed a publishing contract.

Things had gone extremely well. My proposal for a book on the UNIX philosophy was accepted without hesitation. ("So many people need to read this book.") Contract negotiations went smoothly. ("I'd like *n* dollars for an advance." "Okay, you got it.") A reasonable deadline had been set. ("We'll give you an extra couple of months to make it easier on you.") You couldn't have asked for a better situation.

To tell the truth, I was scared to death. After getting over the initial enthusiasm of signing up to author a book on a topic I'd been harping on for years, I ran headlong into a reality that I was mentally unprepared for: I now had to write the darn thing.

My past writing experience consisted of pumping out features for a regional entertainment magazine. I'd learned how to string words together. I knew about topic sentences, action verbs, and the use of passive voice. I could hook a reader and keep him interested. However, writing magazine articles only made me a great sprinter. Now it was time to run the marathon.

The first thing I did was sprint to a friend for advice. An author of several books, he had run this race before. What could I do, I asked, to get a handle on this seemingly insurmountable task?

"Buy a notebook PC," he replied.

Seeing the Neanderthal look on my face, he explained that writing a book is an all-or-nothing proposition. It takes an intense, concentrated effort to put so many thoughts down on paper. You must think about the book nearly always: while brushing your teeth in the morning, while driving to and from work, between meetings, while having lunch, during your workout at the health club, while watching television with the family, and before you go to sleep at night. The notebook PC is the only text entry device at once powerful and portable enough to enable you to write a book just about anywhere.

An amazing feat of modern microtechnology, the typical notebook PC puts most capabilities of a PC compatible in a package thinner than a three-ring binder. Weighing less than seven pounds, its low-profile design makes it as easy to carry around as a college textbook. Most come with hard disk drives and built-in modems, making them viable workhorses for everyday computing tasks such as calculating spreadsheets, word processing, and programming.

Several years ago, Apple Computer ran a television ad showing two executives discussing the merits of various personal computers. Both men were talking about technical specifications when one appeared to have a profound revelation: the most powerful computer is not the one with the fastest CPU, the biggest disk drives, or terrific software. It is the one that is used most.

Judged solely by this criterion, the notebook PC will soon rank as the most powerful computer ever built. It doesn't have the blinding speed of, say, a Cray supercomputer. Nor does it have the storage capacity of the latest disk farm technology. Its graphics capability will probably always lag behind the raciest desktop screens. Hardly the epitome of performance, it has only one real advantage: portability.

This brings us to the next tenet of the UNIX philosophy. You might wish to make a special note of this one. It marks the reason UNIX has nullified the longevity of thousands of man-years' worth of software development effort:

TENET 4
Choose Portability over Efficiency

Software development involves choices, each of which represents a compromise. Sometimes the developer must write a short, simple subroutine because he doesn't have time to include a more sophisticated one. At other times a limited amount of RAM might be a constraint. In some situations one must avoid tying up a network connection with too many small data packets because the network protocol in use favors transfers of large data blocks. The programmer always chooses from a set of compromises in attempting to satisfy often conflicting goals.

One difficult choice the programmer faces is portability versus efficiency. It is an agonizing one, too, because favoring efficiency results in nonportable code, while selecting portability often results in software whose performance is unsatisfactory.

Efficient software performs as fast as the host machine can run it. It takes full advantage of the underlying hardware, often completely disregarding portability issues. It capitalizes on such features as graphics accelerators, cache memories, and specialized floating-point instructions.

Although efficient software is attractive from a purist's standpoint, the value of running the software on many different machine architectures tips the balance in the other direction. The reason is more financial than technical: in today's computing environments, software that runs on only one architecture sharply limits its potential marketability.

Building in portability doesn't mean that you must necessarily settle for inefficient, technically arcane software. To the contrary, obtaining optimum performance from portable software requires a higher level of technical sophistication. If the sophistication isn't there, however, you have an alternative in that you can wait until the hardware becomes available.

Next ——'s hardware will run faster

We used to fill the blank with "year"; i.e., next year's hardware will run faster. Because of the speed at which hardware technology races ahead, today we can sometimes say that even next quarter's hardware may run faster. The ever-shrinking product development cycle of today's computer manufacturers allows them to produce newer models in a fraction of the time they required in the past. Vendors leapfrog each other with frequent announcements of higher performance for a lower price. As a result, whatever computer you're using today will soon feel like the clunky old behemoth in the back of your college lab.

This tendency toward tighter design cycles will accelerate, too. Today's semiconductor designers use sophisticated simulators to create follow-on versions of their microchips. As these simulators—themselves powerful computers—continue to gain speed, developers can complete new designs even faster. These newer chips then become the engines used in tomorrow's simulators. The phenomenon snowballs with each successive generation of silicon processors. The semiconductor design world rides a dizzying, upward-bound performance spiral.

As faster machines replace slower ones, the critical issue then becomes whether your software will run on the newer machines. You might spend days or weeks tuning an application for better performance on today's platform, only to find that the next hardware upgrade gives you a factor of ten increase in speed "free." However, your software must be portable to take advantage of the new higher-performance machine.

In the UNIX environment, this usually translates into writing much software as shell scripts. A shell script consists of multiple executable commands placed in a single file executed indirectly by the UNIX command interpreter. Because of the wide array of small, single-purpose commands found in a typical UNIX distribution, all but the lowest level tasks can be constructed easily from shell scripts.

A side benefit of shell scripts is that they are far more portable than programs written in the C language. This may sound heretical, but writing your programs in C should be considered only if absolutely necessary. In the UNIX environment, C lacks the portability of shell scripts. C programs often depend on definitions in header files, machine architecture sizes, and a host of other nonportable characteristics of a UNIX implementation. As UNIX was ported from 16-bit to 32-bit and 64-bit architectures, a significant amount of software became inoperable because C is not very portable. C is little more than the assembly language of the '80s.

What if you want your program to run on other systems besides UNIX? Then, yes, C is the language of choice at this point in data processing history. Understand, though, that one possibility raised here is that someday UNIX may be the dominant operating system, and those other systems may no longer exist. If this occurs, any program that runs under UNIX will run on more than 90 percent of the world's computers.

Don't spend too much time making a program run faster

If it barely runs fast enough, then accept the fact that it already meets your needs. All time spent tuning subroutines and eliminating critical bottlenecks should be done with an eye toward leveraging performance gains on future hardware platforms as well. Resist the tendency to make the software faster for its own sake. Remember that next year's machine is right around the corner.

A common mistake that many UNIX programmers make is to rewrite a shell script in C to gain a marginal edge in performance. This is a waste of time better spent obtaining constructive responses from users. Sometimes a shell script may not run fast enough. However, if you absolutely must have high performance and believe that you need C to get it, think it over—twice. Certain specialized applications notwithstanding, it usually doesn't pay to rewrite a script in C.

If—and this is a very big "if"—you must optimize a C program's performance, UNIX provides *prof* and other tools for identifying the subroutines used most. Tuning routines called upon hundreds or thousands of times produces the greatest improvement for the least effort.

The most efficient way is rarely portable

Any time a program takes advantage of special hardware capabilities, it becomes at once more efficient and less portable. Special capabilities may occasionally provide great boosts, but their usage requires separate device-dependent code that must be updated when the target hardware is replaced by a faster version. Although updating hardware-specific code provides job security for many system programmers, it does little to enhance the profit margins of their employers.

Earlier in my career I worked on a design team producing an early version of the X Window System on a new hardware platform. An engineer on the project wrote several demos that took advantage of the advanced graphics capabilities in the hardware. Another engineer coded a similar set of demos to run under the portable interface provided by the X Window System. The first engineer's demos really sparkled because they used state-of-the-art graphics accelerators. Incredibly efficient, they flexed the hardware's muscles to their fullest. The second engineer's demos, while admittedly slower, remained staunchly portable because they ran under X.

Eventually, the state-of-the-art graphics hardware became not-so-state-of-the-art. So the company built a faster graphics chip set incompatible with the first. Re-implementing the first engineer's demos for the new hardware required a significant effort, more than anyone had time for. So the demos disappeared into obscurity. The portable demos that ran under X, on the other hand, ported to the new system without modification and are still in use as of this writing.

When you take advantage of specialized hardware capabilities for efficiency's sake, your software becomes a tool for selling the hardware instead of software that stands on its own. This limits its efficacy as a software product and leads you to sell it for less than its intrinsic worth.

Software tightly coupled to a hardware platform holds its value only as long as that platform remains competitive. Once the platform's advantage fades, the software's worth drops off dramatically. For it to retain its value, it must be ported from one platform to another as newer, faster models become available. Failure to move rapidly to the next available hardware spells death. Market opportunity windows remain open for short periods before slamming shut. If the software doesn't appear within its opportunity window, it finds its market position usurped by a competitor. One could even argue that the inability to port their software to the latest platforms has killed more software companies than all other reasons combined.

One measure of an application's success is the number of systems it runs on. Obviously, a program depending largely on one vendor's hardware base will have difficulties becoming a major contender compared to another that has captured the market on multiple vendors' systems. In essence, portable software is more valuable than efficient software.

Software conceived with portability in mind reduces the transfer cost associated with moving to a new platform. Since the developer must spend less time porting, he can devote more time to developing new features that may attract more users and give the product a commercial advantage. Therefore, portable software is more valuable from the day it is written. The incremental effort incurred in making it portable from the beginning pays off handsomely later as well.

Portable software also reduces the need for user training

Once a user has spent the time to learn an application package, he can reap the benefits of this investment on future platforms by running the same package. Future versions of the software may change slightly, but the core idea and the user interface support-ing it are likely to remain intact. The user's experience on the product increases with each new version, transforming him from an "occasional" user into a "power" user over time.

Good programs never die—they are ported to new hardware platforms

Have you ever noticed that certain programs have been around for years in one form or another? People have always found them useful. They have true intrinsic worth. Usually someone has taken it upon himself to write or port them, for fun or profit, to the currently popular hardware platform.

Take EMACS-style text editors, for example. While in some ways they are bad examples of UNIX applications, they have long been favorites with programmers in general and UNIX devotees in particular. You can always find a version around not only on UNIX systems but on MS-DOS and OpenVMS systems as well. Although some EMACS versions have grown into cumbersome monoliths over the years, in its simplest form EMACS still offers a respectable "modeless" vehicle for entering and manipulating text.

Another good example is the electronic spreadsheet, such as Lotus 1-2-3. Although the Lotus product clearly dominates the field, many clones have been written to emulate its capabilities on other machines beside the IBM PC and PC-compatibles. Not all of the features of the original 1-2-3 are found in all of its clones. Still, its core idea—the ability to establish mathematical relationships between "cells" of information—is seen everywhere.

No single individual, company, organization, or nation can keep a good idea to itself. Eventually, others take notice, and "rea-sonable facsimiles" of the idea begin to appear. The intelligent entity, recognizing an idea's merit, should strive to implement it on as many platforms as practical to gain the largest possible market share. The most effective way to achieve this end is to write portable software.

CASE STUDY: THE ATARI 2600

Let's look at the Atari 2600, otherwise known as the Atari Video Computer System. The VCS was the first successful home video game system, a product in the right place at the right time. It captured the imagination of a people that had just sampled Space Invaders at local pubs and arcades and was ready to bring the new world of video games into the living room. The first cartridge-programmable game console, it launched an entire industry bent on bringing the joys of games once found only in campus labs and software professionals' hidden directories to the family television screen. If programmers have an affinity for games, it is minuscule compared to the interests of mainstream America and, for that matter, the world at large.

High on the price-performance curve when it was introduced, the 2600 gave you reasonable capabilities for your money. The 8-bit console sold for around $100 or so. It came with a couple of joysticks and a pair of potentiometers known as "paddle" controllers. Atari supplied it with Combat, a cartridge programmed with a variety of two-person battle games incorporating tanks, jets, or Fokkers.

Atari made comparatively little money on sales of the console. The big profits came from the sale of the game cartridges. With prices ranging from $14 each to more than $35, these units became the bread and butter of Atari and a slew of smaller software houses hoping to capitalize on the video game craze. From Atari's standpoint, once the software engineering investment to develop a cartridge was recovered, the rest was pure gravy.

A friend of mine found a job at a software house that produced cartridges for the 2600. He explained that it was quite a feat to squeeze, say, a chess game or a "shoot-em-up" in less than 8K of EPROM. It was like jamming twenty people into a Volkswagen Bug: not everyone gets a chance to look out the windows.

In writing the code for the game cartridges he wrote some of the most efficient—and nonportable—software in his career. He treated instructions as data and data as instructions. Certain operations were performed during horizontal retrace, the time between when the light beam on a television set finishes painting the last dot on the right side of the screen and it returns to the left side. Every possible shortcut had to be taken to conserve memory. His code was at once a thing of beauty and a software maintainer's worst nightmare.

Sometime during the reign of the 2600, Atari introduced the 800, a 6502-based system that became the flagship of their home computer line. The 800 was a true computer in the sense that it had a typewriter-style keyboard and interfaces for secondary storage and communications devices. Selling for close to $1,000, the 800 posed little threat to the 2600's captive niche—until the price of memory chips dropped.

Because of competitive pressures from other vendors and the 800's popular extended graphics capabilities, Atari fell under heavy pressure to produce a video game machine for the mass market that could run the 800's software. The new machine, dubbed the 5200, made it possible for the mass market computer illiterates to run the same games that the "techies" were playing on the 800.

Once the mass market had discovered this amazing new machine, it dumped the primitive looking 2600 for the smoother graphics of the 5200. The bottom then promptly fell out of Atari 2600 game cartridge prices. Dealers, expecting the demise of the 2600, began slashing the prices on their existing inventories, virtually flooding the market with cut-rate 2600 cartridges. This drove prices down even further, taking down a few software houses in the process. Today 2600 game cartridges sell at garage sales for under $5, if you can find them.

The pain didn't end there for the cartridge producers. Most popular games on the 2600 became instant hits on the 5200 as well—but not before they were completely rewritten to run on the new hardware platform. Since the code in the 2600 cartridges was so efficient, it lacked anything remotely portable. This meant rewriting the software at great expense.

The point here is that, although the game cartridge software was arguably the most efficient ever written, its value plummeted the day the new hardware was announced, all because it was not portable enough to be recompiled and reused on the 5200. Had the code been portable, the video game phenomenon would have evolved quite differently. Atari would probably have become the world's largest supplier of software.

Finally, note that you will pay as little as a few dollars for an Atari 2600 game cartridge today. You still cannot purchase Lotus 1-2-3 for less than several hundred dollars. Part of the reason for this is that Lotus 1-2-3 migrated from one platform to the next as Intel Corporation released progressively more powerful versions of its 8086 processor. This kept 1-2-3 on the leading edge of the power curve. The developers of 1-2-3 have also kept a sharp eye on the future of UNIX. Several years ago they ported 1-2-3 to UNIX, making it portable in the process. Lotus has protected its profit base for years to come.

The moral of the story? Portability pays. Anything else is merely efficient.

Thus far we have been discussing the merits of portable software versus efficient software. Code moved easily to a new platform is far more valuable than code that takes advantage of special hardware features. We have seen that this axiom can be measured in real terms, i.e., in dollars and cents. To preserve its profit base, a software company should strive for portability in its products, possibly foregoing efficiency in the process.

Portable code, however, goes only halfway toward meeting the goal of portability. All software consists of instructions and data. By making the instructions portable, you ensure that your code will be ready to run on next year's machine. What then happens to your data? Is it left behind? Not at all. The UNIX programmer chooses to make not only the code portable but the data as well.

How does one make one's data portable? The next tenet of the UNIX philosophy is one solution:

TENET 5
Store Numerical Data in Flat ASCII Files

"Flat ASCII files" means that you store all numerical data as ASCII text. Period. Binary format files are verböten. No special filesystem formats are allowed. This rules out a host of interesting but nonportable formats invented by vendors for proprietary purposes. Data files should consist of only a stream of bytes separated by line feed characters or "newlines," in the lingo of the UNIX world.

Many consider this a bitter pill to swallow, but UNIX programmers swear that this is the best way. Here is the secret: while data is kept on whatever kind of storage media, eventually it must go somewhere. Data sitting on a disk diminishes in value. For data to remain alive and valuable, it must move occasionally. Otherwise it should be archived and deleted.

Data that goes nowhere is dead data.

If you expect to move your data easily, you must make it portable. Any impediments to data movement, whether unintentional or by design, place limits on your data's potential value. The longer your data must sit somewhere, the less it will be worth when it finally arrives. The problem is, if your data is not in a format that is useful to its destination, it must be converted. That conversion process takes time. Every second spent in data conversion eats away at your data's worth.

CNN, the Cable News Network, won top honors in 1991 for its coverage of the Persian Gulf War. They provided the world with graphic scenes of the conflict and they did it quickly. Many people rushed home to their television sets every night to watch the events unfold. Would the CNN coverage have been as riveting if they spent several days converting the videotape from beta to VHS, airmailed the tapes to Atlanta, and showed them only during prime time?

So it is with your data. If it takes extra time to convert your data from a nonportable format to move it, the data will not be worth as much when it gets there. The world moves much too quickly to wait for your data.

ASCII text is a common interchange format

It's not necessarily the best format, only the most common one. Other formats, such as EBCDIC, have been used in some applications, but none has found such wide acceptance as ASCII. In nearly all cases, data encoded in ASCII can be handled by target platforms.

By using ASCII, you eliminate the difficulties of converting your data from one binary format to another. Few binary formats are standardized. Each vendor has defined its own binary encoding, and most of them are different. Converting from one vendor's format to another's can be an arduous task requiring anywhere from several days to several months. This time would be much better spent using the data.

ASCII text is easily read and edited

This makes it possible for you to examine the data without conversion tools. If the data doesn't look right, you can use a standard text editor to modify it. Specialized tools are not required. You don't need a separate editor for each kind of data file. One size fits all.

The real power of ASCII text files becomes apparent when developing programs that use pipes under UNIX. The pipe is a mechanism for passing one program's output to another's input without using a temporary file. Many UNIX programs are little more than a collection of smaller programs joined by a series of pipes. As developers prototype a program, they can easily check the data for accuracy at each point along the pipeline. If there is a problem, they can interrupt the flow through the pipeline and figure out whether the data or its manipulator is the problem. This greatly speeds up the development process, giving the UNIX programmer a significant edge over programmers on other operating systems.

ASCII text files also simplify the UNIX user's interface with the system. Most administrative information under UNIX is kept in flat ASCII files and made available for universal inspection. This significantly reduces the amount of time spent by individuals in accessing the information to accomplish their daily work. Information about other users, systems on the network, and general statistics can be gleaned with minimal effort. Ironically, portability here results in greater efficiency.

ASCII data files simplify
the use of UNIX text tools

Most UNIX environments contain dozens of utilities for transmitting, modifying, and filtering text. UNIX users employ these utilities in many combinations to do their daily work. Here are some more popular ones along with a brief description of their functions:

awk	Perform functions on text arranged in fields
cut	Extract specific columns from lines of text
diff	Perform a line-by-line comparison of two text files
expand	Convert tab stops to spaces
expr	Extract part of a string from another string
fmt	A simple paragraph formatter
grep	Extract lines from a file containing a specified text string
head	Display the first n lines of a file
lex	Perform lexical analysis of a text stream
more	Display a text file one screenful at a time

paste	Convert a single text column into multiple columns
roff	A comprehensive text formatter and typesetter
sed	A noninteractive text line editor
sort	Sort a column of text
tail	Display the last *n* lines of a file
test	Compare two strings for equality
tr	Replace selected characters in a file
wc	Count the number of lines, words, or characters in a file

Many of these utilities have other features besides those mentioned in the list. For example, *awk* can mix alphabetical and numeric text interchangeably. *Test* can check the modes of files to learn whether they are writable by the user. *Lex* provides an interface to the C programming language driven by matching string expressions in the input stream. *Sed* by itself is powerful enough to replace commands like *grep*, *head*, and *tail*.

The mixed-mode capabilities of these commands tend to blur the line between text and what is traditionally thought of as data. Hence, it makes it easier to represent in textual form that which was formerly stored in binary files. UNIX programmers usually store numerical data in text files because the UNIX environment provides a rich set of tools to manipulate those files.

The idea of data stored as text combined with a diverse set of text manipulation tools makes UNIX a formidable data processor. This is why UNIX is a strong contender to become the world's operating system. It's not because it's perfect—UNIX devotees attest that it is not. Nor is it because many people use it—they don't. It's just that it is so easy to move around data stored as text. Even people who aren't programmers find it easy to read and interpret data stored in flat ASCII files.

The developers of Digital's OpenVMS may be right in thinking that most people are afraid of the computer. Instead of shielding users from the system, though, UNIX takes them inside it. It leads them through labyrinthine logic trails while they hold onto their last vestige of familiarity, namely, their data in a format that can be read and understood. For all the criticism of the "un-friendly UNIX user interface," UNIX may well be the friendliest system of all. Users can always look at their data without having to be system gurus skilled at interpreting complex binary file formats.

Increased portability overcomes the lack of speed

Throughout this discussion, you've probably been thinking, "Yeah, portability is nice, but what about performance?" It's true that using flat ASCII text files slows things down a bit. It takes two or three ASCII characters to represent the contents of one binary byte. So you're talking about potentially a 3:1 reduction in performance. This sounds significant but it really isn't in all except high-resolution real-time applications.

Eventually, every application program is ported to a new system or else it becomes extinct. The unrelenting progress of computer manufacturers assures us that what may have been prohibitively expensive today will be dirt cheap tomorrow. It doesn't pay to run an application on a slow system that is becoming increasingly costly to maintain.

The payoff in using ASCII text comes when you must port your application to a new architecture. If you had enough fore-sight to make your program portable, then with ASCII text it becomes a trivial matter to move your data to a new platform as well. Woe to software engineers who must port both data and program code. Their data will be stale by the time it ever sees the new memory boards. The cumulative time lost by a 3:1 performance reduction pales in comparison to the weeks or months lost in moving the data to the new platform.

The lack of speed is overcome by next year's machine

Again, we've acknowledged that ASCII text files pose a drag on performance. You could possibly realize up to a 3:1 reduction in speed. However, if the application meets today's minimum performance requirements, you can expect that next year's machine will yield a dramatic improvement—if your data can be ported.

As of this writing, next year's machine usually offers enough additional computing power to render any of today's performance concerns about ASCII text files superfluous. In other words, if your application barely performs adequately today, its speed will be ample tomorrow. In a few years you may even have to start thinking about how to slow it down so people can use it!

CASE STUDY: ONE UNIX PHILOSOPHER'S BAG OF TRICKS

We have seen that given a choice between high efficiency and high portability, UNIX programmers' preference weighs heavily on the latter. As a result, their applications are often among the first to run on new platforms as they become available. This gives their software a definite edge in the marketplace. In a world where windows of opportunity open overnight and slam shut as little as a month later, pursuing the portability priority can mean the difference between being an industry leader and the others that wish they were.

How did UNIX programmers come to embrace such beliefs? Most software engineers weren't taught the importance of portability in school, at least not with any sense of conviction. More likely, they learned the value of portable code and data the best way: through firsthand experience.

Most UNIX "gurus," as they're called, carry a collection of programs and shell scripts that make up their personal tool kit. These tools have followed them as they've moved from machine to machine, job to job, and company to company. For purposes of illustration, let's look at a UNIX philosopher's bag of tricks.

My personal collection of tools has varied through the years. Here is a partial sample of those that have stood the tests of time and portability.

cal   A shell script front end to the UNIX *cal* program that allows you to specify textual names for months instead of numbers. Borrowed from *The UNIX Programming Environment* by Brian Kernighan and Rob Pike.[*]

cp   A "fumble finger" front end to the UNIX *cp* program that prevents you from unintentionally overwriting an existing file

l   Runs the *ls* command with the -F switch specified

ll   Runs the *ls* command with the -l switch specified

mv   Similar to the *cp* script, it prevents you from unintentionally overwriting an existing file by renaming another file to a file with the same name

vit   Invokes the *vi* editor with the -t flag for use with tags and a tags file. Tags make it easy to locate subroutines in a collection of files.

I have converted some scripts into aliases for use with the C shell, an interactive command interpreter originally found on Berkeley UNIX systems. Aliases allow you to specify alternate forms of heavily used commands without having to resort to putting everything in shell scripts. Like shell scripts, they, too, are portable.

I originally built these tools under UNIX Version 7 on a Digital PDP-11/70 at a small company engaged in the manufacture of newspaper composition systems. As the company added new systems for software development, I moved them to PDP-11/34, PDP-11/44, and LSI-11/23 systems also running UNIX. This doesn't sound like a grand feat, given the renowned compatibility of the PDP-11 line, but wait. It gets better.

Eventually I left the company in pursuit of other career opportunities, taking my tools with me on a nine-track tape. The C programs and shell scripts soon found a home on a Digital VAX 750. The VAX 750 had more horsepower than the smaller PDP-11s I'd been using. Consequently, they ran a bit faster at the new company. They picked up even more speed when the company

---

[*] © 1984, Bell Telephone Laboratories, Inc.

replaced the VAX 750 with a VAX 780. All this happened without any modifications to the tools whatsoever.

About that time, workstations—those wondrous you-mean-I-can-have-the-whole-darn-computer-to-myself boxes—vaulted onto the scene. Everyone flocked to buy the hot new machines from Sun Microsystems, my employer included. So the tools moved from the PDP-11 to the VAX line suddenly found themselves running without modification on Sun workstations.

Having spent the greater part of my career in New England, I found the latest equipment from the original digital equipment maker to be fairly common within a hundred miles of Boston. Again I ported my old reliable C programs and shell scripts to the Digital line, this time to the VAX 8600 series and later to the VAX 8800 series. Again, the tools ran without modification.

Necessity is the mother of midnight invention. A software engineer I was working with had noticed a large cache of Digital Professional 350s collecting dust in a warehouse. An enterprising individual concluded that these 350s would make fine personal computers for us at home, especially if they were running UNIX. So he proceeded to port a version of UNIX to the 350. My tools soon followed.

Then along came the parade of VAXstations and the early versions of the X Window System. A portable window system was a major step in the evolution of useful user interfaces. Despite all the whiz-bang effects of a window system, I still found that my favorite tools were very helpful in an *xterm* window (terminal emulator).

But the computer business is a risky business. You must remain flexible to stay on top. To a software engineer, flexibility translates into portability. If your software does not port to the newest machine, it will die. Period. So when the RISC-based DECstation 3100s and 5000s came along, it was a port-or-die situation. My tools displayed their penchant for portability again.

As of this writing, my little bag of tricks is currently running on the world's first 64-bit commercial microprocessor—without modification.

These C programs and shell scripts have seen more than ten years of daily usage, on different vendors' machines, under a variety of UNIX versions, on everything from 16-bit to 32-bit to 64-bit CPU architectures running the gamut from PCs to minicomputers to mainframes. How many other programs do you know of that have been used for so long in so many environments?

My experience with these tools is hardly the exception. UNIX programmers the world over have similar stories to tell. Nearly everyone who has used UNIX on more than a casual basis has their own collection of "goodies." Some undoubtedly have far more comprehensive tool kits than mine. Others have probably ported their software to even greater numbers of platforms, all without modification and with virtually no user retraining.

The record of portability speaks for itself. By making your programs and data easy to port, you build long-lasting, tangible value into your software. It's that simple. Code and data that opt for efficiency lock themselves into the architecture for which they were designed. With the onrush of new platforms, obsolescence preys on the nonportable. Instead of watching the worth of your software investment shrink to zero with each industry announcement, plan ahead. Design with portability in mind.

When the 1,000,000 MIPS machine arrives on your desktop—and this may be sooner than you think—be sure your software will be ready for it.

5

Now THAT'S Leverage!

Be fruitful and multiply.

GENESIS 1:28

If you want to make a lot of money, sell Tupperware. You know, those plastic storage containers that seal in freshness and fill your fridge with scads of hopelessly unlabeled pastel bowls. The next time you wish you had another six feet of kitchen cabinets, consider how their universal appeal has made them a household fixture. Everyone has at least one Tupperware piece tucked away somewhere.

Individual dealers sell Tupperware products via the "party plan." They stage informal gatherings at the homes of people who sponsor them in return for a nominal share of the proceeds. They stay busy at these parties, giving product demonstrations, offering hints and tips, taking orders. It's hard work. A few of them even make a little money at it.

My aunt sold almost a million dollars' worth of Tupperware products one year.

When I heard this, my first thought was "That's a lot of bowls!" After getting used to the idea that we would soon have a millionaire in the family, I started wondering how she had done it. She was just a "regular" person. You know, one of the family. Hardly the type you would expect to be well on her way to riches.

I knew she had worked very hard, continually soaring to new heights with her seemingly limitless energy. Everywhere she went she would talk up a storm about how good Tupperware products were. Sometimes she would visit our house while on vacation and she would toil very late, catching up on her business paperwork.

Still, for all her grueling determination, it just didn't fit. The math simply did not work out. Suppose that a bowl sold for an average price of $7. To sell a million dollars' worth would require selling 142,858 of them. If you assume that she worked six days a week for fifty weeks, then she would have to have sold 477 bowls a day.

Now, my aunt is a terrific salesperson. Her sales prowess is legendary. If it can be sold, she can offer it to you and you will buy it. But 477 bowls a day, every day (except Sunday), was more than I thought even she could do. After all, one has to rest occasionally. Besides, she was raising a family at the time.

So one day I pulled her aside and asked her how she sold a million dollars' worth of Tupperware products in one year. Her reply? "Silly! I didn't sell all those bowls. I got someone to sell them for me!"

She explained that she started out selling Tupperware at home parties on weeknights. On a good week, she figured, she could do five parties and sell between $100 and $150 worth at each. Eventually she realized that, while she was a fine plastics peddler, there were only so many hours in the week in which to peddle. So she found twenty other people and sold them on the idea of selling Tupperware. Each of them would hold five parties weekly, making a total of one hundred a week between them. She would sell her bowls to those twenty people for a small profit from each. It wasn't long before those twenty people understood the value of "pyramiding" themselves. Soon some had twenty people selling bowls for each of them.

The rest is multilevel marketing history.

Then my aunt shared a potent bit of wisdom: no matter how bright, energetic, or aggressive you are, there is only so much of "you" to go around. If you want to be fantastically successful, then you must multiply your effect on the world. It's not enough to have a high IQ or the ability to sell winter parkas in Hawaii. You need to set enterprises in motion that distribute and enhance the impact of your talents and abilities. For every hour of your labor, expect a yield of five, a hundred, or even a thousand times your efforts.

The key word here is leverage. Like the lever and fulcrum you studied in high school physics class, any movement at one end of the lever is experienced at the other end. If the fulcrum is placed in the exact center of the lever, a one-to-one correspondence exists between the opposite ends of the lever. If one end moves up n units, then the other end goes down by the same number of units. However, if you stand at one end of the lever and place the fulcrum close to you, a small movement at your end can effect a much larger motion at the opposite end. The trick, then, is to find a way to move the fulcrum closer to you in an endeavor. In other words, you want a one-inch move on your end of the lever to send the other end halfway to the moon.

One reason for the growing success of UNIX is its ability to help the leveraging efforts of individuals. This didn't just happen as a matter of chance. It came about by way of cooperative design by dozens and later hundreds of programmers. They recognized that they could only do so much by themselves. But if they could multiply their effects, they could take advantage of "software leverage."

TENET 6
Use Software Leverage to Your Advantage

Let's suppose you're one of the world's best programmers. Every piece of code you write turns to gold. Your applications become instant hits the day they're released. Critics shower your work with praise and your software adorns the covers of the trade rags. Your programs are truly unique.

Unfortunately, "one of a kind" poses a problem for you. The same uniqueness that distinguishes your work also becomes the chain that binds you. If you do all of the work yourself, you can only do so much. Unless you can find a way to off-load some of it, you will burn yourself out long before you achieve your maximum potential.

Good programmers write good code; great programmers "borrow" good code

The best way to write lots of software is to borrow it. By borrowing software we mean incorporating other people's modules, programs, and configuration files into your applications. In producing a derivative work, you augment the previous developers' efforts, carrying their implementations to new heights of utility. Their software becomes more valuable as it finds a home in more applications; your software becomes more valuable because your investment in it has been reduced relative to its return. It's a mutually beneficial situation.

Although you may have lowered your investment in an application, you must not necessarily settle for reduced profits. Applications built by integrating other people's code can sell for considerable amounts of money. They also tend to grab significant market share because they usually reach the market before those developed by competitors. The old adage "the early bird gets the worm" holds especially true here. If you can be the first with a hot new application, it doesn't matter that you achieved your position by using other people's work. Potential customers just want to know whether your software can do the job. They are less interested in how your software works than in what it can do for them.

Leveraging other people's code can result in powerful advantages for the individual programmer, too. Some programmers believe that they protect their job security by writing the code themselves. "Since I write good code, I'll always have a job," they reason. The problem is, writing good code takes time. If you have to write every line of code used in an application, you will appear slow and inefficient. The real job security belongs to the software developer who can cut and paste modules together quickly and efficiently. Developers like that often produce so much software in a short time that companies generally consider them indispensable.

I recall a less-than-top-notch software engineer who couldn't program his way out of a paper bag, as the saying goes. He had a knack, however, for knitting lots of little modules together. He hardly ever wrote any of them himself, though. He would just fish around in the system's directories and source code repositories all day long, sniffing for routines he could string together to make a complete program. Heaven forbid that he should have to write any code. Oddly enough, it wasn't long before management recognized him as an outstanding software engineer, someone who could deliver projects on time and within budget. Most of his peers never realized that he had difficulty writing even a rudimentary sort routine. Nevertheless, he became enormously successful by simply using whatever resources were available to him.

Avoid the not-invented-here syndrome

Symptoms of NIH appear in the finest of organizations. When a group refuses to recognize the value of another group's application, ... when one would prefer to write an application from scratch instead of using one "off the shelf,". . . when software written elsewhere isn't used simply because it was written elsewhere, . . . NIH is at work.

Contrary to popular belief, NIH does not expand creativity. Viewing another's work and declaring that you could do it better doesn't necessarily make you more creative. If you start from scratch and redesign an existing application, you're engaging in imitation, not creativity. By avoiding NIH, however, you open doors to new and exciting worlds of engineering design. Since less time is spent rewriting existing routines, you can devote more time to developing new functional capabilities. It's like starting out a Monopoly game owning hotels on Boardwalk and Park Place. You don't have to spend half the game trying to build the hotels.

NIH can be especially dangerous with today's emphasis on standardization in the software industry. Standards drive software vendors toward commoditization. All spreadsheets begin to look alike, all word processors provide the same capabilities, and so on. The resulting oversupply of available software to accomplish everyday tasks drives prices down, thus limiting profitability. Every vendor needs a spreadsheet, a word processor, and so on, just to stay in the game. But few vendors can afford to produce those staples from scratch. The most successful companies will be those that "borrow" the software, leaving them the opportunity to create enhancements or "added value," in industry jargon.

I once worked with a team of software engineers who were working on a graphical user interface for a window system. We had an idea to mimic another popular interface on the market. Since the other was so successful, we reasoned, then ours would surely be a hit as well. The plan was to rewrite the user interface from scratch, making it more efficient in the process.

We had two obvious strikes against us. First, in attempting to write a more efficient program, we would have to take some steps that would result in nonportable software. By "hardwiring" the application to our target architecture, we severely limited the size of our potential market. Second, it would take several months to write the user interface from scratch. While we were busy writing our own user interface, the developers of the one we were imitating weren't exactly twiddling their thumbs. They were busy adding features and enhancements to their software. By the time we released our version, theirs would be at least a generation removed from ours.

Fortunately for us, we were too blind then to realize that the other company's user interface would have evolved considerably while we were developing ours. Instead we became concerned that we might become involved in a patent infringement suit if our software looked and felt too much like the one we were bent on imitating. So we ran our ideas past one of our corporate lawyers. He opened our eyes to a more interesting possibility.

"Instead of duplicating the other company's work, why not use their software in our product?" he asked. We all took a deep swallow on that one, and the letters P-R-I-D-E got stuck in our throats. His suggestion dealt a real blow to the NIH tradition we had carefully nurtured and guarded over the years. The toughest part was admitting that his idea made much sense.

So we set about learning how to incorporate and enhance the other vendor's software in our own product. It was a painful endeavor, given our history of wanting to do it our own way. Eventually we released a set of programs built using the other software as a base. The result? Customers praised our efforts at compatibility. They bought our product because it offered value above and beyond competitors' packages while remaining compatible with de facto industry standards. We had a winner on our hands.

Take note of the phrase "added value," for it holds the key to success in the software realm of the 90s and beyond. As computer hardware has become a commodity, so software will proceed down the same path. The various ongoing standardization efforts virtually guarantee this. Prices of software will drop, since every major vendor will be providing similar capabilities. Software companies will then have two options: watch their profit margins shrink to zero or else preserve them by adding value to standard applications. They must invent features that differentiate their products from industry standards as they simultaneously retain compatibility with those same standards. To survive, companies must meet the challenge of conflicting goals of uniformity and independence. The only way to win will be to add glitter to the wheel, not reinvent it.

The CD-ROM may pose the biggest threat of all to the bastions of NIH adherents. These same shiny disks used to distribute the latest Michael Jackson tunes can also store over five hundred megabytes of programs and data cheaply. An inexpensive medium such as this has the potential to permanently alter the software landscape. With the introduction of the CD, storage technology has taken an irreversible leap forward.

In a recent visit to a local PC shop, I discovered a compact disk containing over twenty-four hundred programs selling for a mere $200. (Yes, it will probably cost $10 by the time you read this, but that only sharpens the point we're trying to make here.) It will be difficult to justify rewriting software available for eight cents elsewhere—unless you're a software developer who can live for months on eight cents.

Allow other people to use your code to leverage their own work

Software engineers frequently tend to hoard their source code. It's as if they believe they have written a unique contrivance, a magic formula that would change the world whose secret they alone possess. They harbor subconscious fears that if they give the source away, they will no longer control this mysterious pearl of great price.

First, software is no magic formula. Anyone with a reasonably logical mind can write the stuff. You can be clever or trite, but all software boils down to a series of calculated statements that cause the hardware to perform certain well-defined operations. A programmer who has never seen the source code can disassemble even the best program. Disassembly is a slow, tedious process, but it can be done.

What about the question of control? A commonly held belief in the computer world is that whoever controls the source code "owns" the program. This is partly true. A company that holds the source code exercises some authority over who modifies a program, who can obtain runtime licenses for it, and so on. Unfortunately, this ability to control the life of a piece of software only protects the company's temporal investment in the program's development, not the software itself. It cannot prevent the onset of imitators ("clones") that seek to emulate its features and functions. Most ideas that are good enough for a company to invest in are also good enough for its competitors to invest in. It's only a matter of time before imitations appear as other vendors strive to catch the wave. The most successful software then becomes the one that appears on the most computers. Companies operating in a proprietary fashion find themselves at a significant disadvantage here.

UNIX owes much of its success to the fact that its developers saw no particular need to retain strong control of its source code. Most people believed it lacked any real value. They regarded UNIX as a curious oddity, suitable for research labs and universities but not much else. No one—except its developers—considered it a serious operating system. Consequently, one could obtain its source code for a pittance.

Soaring development costs caused hardware vendors to reduce their investment in the software needed to make their platforms marketable. A pittance for an operating system soon looked like a very good deal. UNIX flourished as a result. Whenever anyone wanted to save the expense of developing an operating system for a new computer, they turned to UNIX. Even today many still consider it among the least expensive operating systems available.

Its low cost has made UNIX the platform of choice for many software houses today. By building on the functional capabilities provided by the UNIX system developers, these companies use software leverage to tremendous advantage. In avoiding the cost of writing an operating system, they can focus instead on enhancing their applications. This puts them in a stronger position in the software world than those companies that must first invest in operating system development before they can produce applications.

Automate everything

One powerful way to use software leverage to your advantage is to make your machines work harder. Any process you do manually today that your computer can do is a waste of your time. Even in modern engineering labs, surprisingly many skilled personnel still rely on crude, manual methods to accomplish their daily tasks. They ought to know better, but old habits die hard. Here are some clues that you may be working harder than necessary—while your computer sits around with little to do:

- Do you use hardcopy often? Once data or text is printed on paper, managing it becomes a manual process. This is terribly inefficient, not to mention a waste of paper. Traditional-style corporate managers often fall into this trap.
- Do you sort data or count lines and objects manually? Most operating environments and especially UNIX provide tools to perform these tasks much faster than you can.
- How do you find files on the system? Do you locate them by perusing your directories one by one? Or do you create a list of your files and scan it with an editor or a browsing tool?
- When trying to find a particular item in a file, do you scan the file manually, relying on your eyes to lead you to the right place? Or do you employ a browser or editor and let the system do the scanning for you?
- Do you use a history mechanism if your command interpreter provides one? A history mechanism allows you to invoke previous commands through a shorthand method. The UNIX shell *csh* is especially good in this regard.
- If you have a workstation with multiple-window capability, do you use only one window at a time? You benefit most by opening two or more windows simultaneously. You can target one window where you work (edit, compile, etc.) The other becomes your test space.
- Do you use a mouse? How often do you use cut-and-paste facilities? If you find yourself frequently entering long strings manually, you're probably not making the most of your mouse. One person I know keeps a window on the screen containing frequently used strings. He cuts

the strings from the window and pastes them in other windows as he needs them, saving much typing.

- Does the command interpreter you use provide command and/or file completion capabilities? Do you use them to accelerate your input, saving you from having to enter many additional keystrokes?

The use of software leverage through increased automation can result in huge productivity gains. I once worked at a place where a significant part of the job involved culling small amounts of information from a diverse collection of sources. In a study we conducted, we observed that each individual was spending as much as twenty hours a week locating the necessary data. This number did not consider the time spent reading and verifying the information once it had been located either. A simple tool was written to index information from the wide variety of sources for rapid retrieval. The payoff? People using the tool spent as little as three hours a week locating the same data that couldn't be found in more than fifteen hours before. Office productivity soared. Everyone was excited. What was once a cumbersome research job was now a painless, highly interactive series of queries carried out by machines. This freed up our time to tackle tougher problems that the machines could not handle.

Every time you automate a task you experience the same kind of leverage that my aunt enjoyed when she found others to sell Tupperware for her. Each command procedure, every program you invoke sends your computer off on a wild spree to complete a task. Instead of convincing people to do your bidding, you direct a well-tuned machine to carry out certain procedures according to instructions you specify. The faster the machine, the bigger the leverage. And, of course, a machine never gets tired or demands a larger percentage of the profits.

In the first part of this chapter we explored some principles concerning the use of leverage, both from a general standpoint and specifically with respect to how leverage applies to software. We have seen how it is important to become a "software scavenger" with an eye toward leveraging the work of others. After discussing the troublesome NIH syndrome, we stressed the value of sharing your work. Finally, we touched upon the obvious but often overlooked desirability of using the computer to automate daily tasks as much as possible.

Now that we have laid a foundation, it's time to build upon that foundation with another element of UNIX, the shell script. Shell scripts capitalize on software leverage in interesting ways. They make it easy for both naive and expert users to tap into the incredible potential found in UNIX. Experienced UNIX programmers use them religiously. You should, too.

Shell scripts bear some resemblance to other command interpreters and control mechanisms, such as batch files under MS-DOS and DCL command files under OpenVMS. Unlike these other implementations, however, UNIX shell scripts exist in an environment ideally suited for indirect command execution. To highlight their significance, we include a special tenet in the UNIX philosophy for them:

TENET 7
Use Shell Scripts to Increase
Leverage and Portability

If you want to take full advantage of software leverage, you need to learn how to use shell scripts effectively. We're not going to show you how to use them here. There are already plenty of books on the subject. Most will show you how to use them. Instead we're going to focus on why you should use them.

Before entering into this discussion, I must caution you that many UNIX kernel programmers regard shell script programmers with disdain. They believe that writing shell scripts is not "the macho thing to do." Some even equate "experienced shell programmer" with "lightweight UNIX type." My guess is that they're simply jealous because writing shell scripts doesn't involve much cerebral pain. Or perhaps it's because you cannot use shell scripts in the kernel. Maybe someone will write a UNIX kernel that will allow shell scripts to be used in the kernel itself someday. Then they, too, can more fully appreciate the benefits of software leverage.

In examining the case for shell scripts, you may get the impression that the author is "anti-C," i.e., programs should never be written in a portable language such as C. If so, you're missing the point. C—and its offspring C++—is a language of choice today. There are times when writing a program in C instead of the shell makes perfect sense. But those times occur much less often than one might suspect. With the popularity of the C language today, it's easy to fall into the trap of bypassing the shell and writing all software in the "assembly language of the 80s." This section will make you aware of the shell alternative, if it doesn't change your mind altogether.

Shell scripts give you awesome leverage

Shell scripts consist of one or more statements that specify C programs and other shell scripts to execute. They run these programs indirectly by loading each command into memory and executing it. Depending on the kind of statement, the top-level shell program may or may not choose to wait for individual commands to complete. The executed commands have been compiled from as many as a hundred, a thousand, or even a hundred thousand lines of C source code, most of which you did not write. Someone else took the time to code and debug those programs. Your shell script is merely the beneficiary, and it uses those lines of code to good advantage. Although you have expended comparatively little effort on your part, you gain the benefit of as much as a million or more lines of code. Now that's leverage.

In the multilevel marketing of plastic housewares, the trick is to get other people to do much of the work for you. You're trying to create a situation where someone else sows and you reap part of the reward. Shell scripts provide that opportunity. They give you the chance to incorporate the efforts of others to meet your goals. You don't write most of the code used in a shell script because someone else has already done it for you.

Let's look at an example. Suppose you wanted a command to list the names of a system's users on a single line. To make it more interesting, let's separate each user's name by commas and display each name only once, no matter how many sessions a user may have opened on the system. This is how our command might look as a shell script written in the Bourne shell, a standard UNIX command interpreter:

```
echo `who | awk '{print $1}' | sort | uniq` | sed 's/ /, /g'
```

Although this shell script consists of a single line, it invokes six different executables: *echo, who, awk, sort, uniq,* and *sed*. These commands are run simultaneously in a kind of series-parallel progression. Except for the *who* command, which starts the sequence, each command receives its data from the previous command in the series and sends its output to the next command in the series. Several UNIX pipes, denoted by ' | ' characters, manage the data transfer. The final command in the sequence, *sed*, sends its output to the user's terminal.

Each command works together synergistically to produce the final output. The *who* command produces a columnar list of the users on the system. It feeds this to *awk* via the pipe mechanism. The first column in the output from *who* contains the names of the users. The *awk* command saves this column and throws away the rest of the data generated by *who*. The list of users is then sent to *sort*, which places them in alphabetical order. The *uniq* command discards any duplicate names caused by users who may have logged in on several sessions at once.

Now we have a sorted list of names, separated by "newlines," the UNIX end-of-line or line feed characters. This list is then sent to the *echo* command via a "back quoting" mechanism that places the output of the previous commands on the echo command line. The Bourne shell's semantics here dictate that single spaces replace all newlines. Finally, our string of user names separated by spaces is sent to the *sed* command where the spaces are converted to commas.

While this might seem quite amazing if you have never seen a UNIX system before, it is a typical UNIX-style command execution. It is not unusual to invoke multiple commands from a single command line in a shell script.

How much code was executed here? The shell script writer took less than a minute to write the script. Others wrote the commands invoked by the script. Under one version of UNIX widely available today, the six commands used contain the following numbers of source code lines:

echo	177
who	755
awk	3,412
sort	2,614
uniq	302
sed	2,093
Total:	9,353

One line in this shell script executes the equivalent of 9,353 lines of source code! Although not an extraordinary amount, this many lines are enough to prove our point. We have increased our power by a factor of 9,353 to one. Again, we have leverage.

This was a simple example of a shell script. Some shell scripts today span several dozen pages containing hundreds of command lines. When you account for the C code behind each executable, the numbers really start to add up. The resulting leverage boggles the mind. As we shall see later, this phenomenon even impressed Albert Einstein.

Shell scripts leverage your time, too

Shell scripts have an intrinsic advantage in that they are interpreted rather than compiled. In a standard C language development environment, the sequence of events goes like this:

THINK-EDIT-COMPILE-TEST

The shell script developer's environment involves one less step:

THINK-EDIT-TEST

The shell script developer bypasses the COMPILE step. This may not seem like a big win given today's highly optimized compilers. Used with speedy RISC processors, such compilers can turn source code into binaries in the blink of an eye. But today's software build environments lean toward complexity. What used to take a few seconds to compile on a fast machine may now take a minute or more because of increasing levels of indirection. Larger programs can take an hour or two. Complete operating systems and their related commands can require an entire day to build.

In skipping the compilation step, the script writers remain focused on the developmental effort. They don't need to go for coffee or read mail while waiting for the command build to complete. Proceeding immediately from EDIT to TEST, they don't have the opportunity to lose a train of thought while waiting for the compiler to finish. This greatly accelerates the software development process.

There is an advantage the C programmer has over the shell script author, namely, an enhanced set of tools for debugging. While developers have created a respectable amount of diagnostic software for the C language, the choices of debugging tools for script writers are severely limited. To date no full-featured debugger for shell scripts has emerged. Shell script writers must still rely on primitive mechanisms such as "sh -x" to display the names of the commands as they execute. Convenient breakpoint facilities are nonexistent. Examining variables is a tedious process. One could argue that, given the ease of shell programming, more comprehensive debugging facilities are unnecessary. I suspect that most shell script writers would disagree.

Shell scripts are more portable than C

A sure way to leverage your software is to make it portable. Earlier we learned that it is important that you share your software with others. Any program moved easily from one platform to another is likely to be used by many people. The more people using your software, the greater the leverage.

In the UNIX environment, shell scripts generally represent the highest level of portability. Most scripts that work on one UNIX system are likely to work on another with little or no modification. Since they are interpreted, it is not necessary to compile them or otherwise transform them for use. It is possible to make a shell script nonportable by design, but such instances are rare and usually not encouraged.

Shell scripts also tend to lack the stigma of "ownership" commonly associated with C source code. People rarely become protective over them. Since they are plainly visible to everyone, no one considers it their corporate duty to protect their contents. Still, a measure of caution is in order here. Copyright laws in the United States and other countries provide protection for shell scripts.

Resist the desire to rewrite shell scripts in C

In the chapter on portability, you were urged not to rewrite shell scripts in C because Next Year's Machine would make them run faster. Since shell scripts are usually highly portable, moving them to Next Year's Machine generally involves virtually no effort. You copy them to the new machine and they run. Period. No mess, no fuss.

Unfortunately, the ability to leave well enough alone is not a virtue found in programmers. If programmers can find a spare moment to tinker with a shell script, you can bet that they will: (a) add some new features to it; (b) attempt to make it run faster by refining the script itself; or (c) try to improve its performance by rewriting part or most of it in C. Can you guess which is most tempting?

The desire to rewrite shell scripts in C stems from the belief that C programs run faster than shell scripts. This eats away at the programmer's desire for a neat, orderly world where everything is well tuned and highly efficient. It's an ego thing. He knows he could have written it in C, and it would have run faster from the beginning. For whatever reason, he didn't. Guilt sets in. If you ask him why he chose to write a program as a shell script, he'll mumble something like "It was all I had time for." He'll follow this excuse with a promise that, when he gets more time, he will rewrite it in C.

It's doubtful that he will ever get the chance. Any programmer worth his salary will be much too busy to go back and rewrite a shell script that already works well enough to meet the needs of its users. Life is much too short for that.

Furthermore, the belief that C programs run faster than shell scripts bears some scrutiny. In the first place, a shell script invokes C programs to accomplish its task. Once the C programs are loaded for execution, then "pure" C programs enjoy no performance advantage over those called from within a script. Most UNIX systems today have tuned the command execution routines so well that the time required to load a program for execution is relatively small compared to the time to perform the complete task.

If you really want your shell scripts to run fast, then you must look into different ways of solving a problem. Too often users and programmers fall into a rut like "that's the way I've always done it, and that's the way I'll always do it." Instead, you need to train yourself to overlook the obvious approaches and find techniques that use the available resources in novel ways.

By way of example, let's look at a situation I ran into a few years ago. I was working in an environment where I received between fifty and a hundred pieces of electronic mail each day, or about three hundred per week. Although I could read and delete some messages, I had to save others for future reference. It wasn't long before I had over two thousand mail messages spread across a hundred directories on my UNIX system. Accessing the right one quickly was becoming difficult.

The obvious solution would be to use the UNIX *grep* command to locate each message based on searching its contents for a particular text string. The problem with this approach was that it was very time consuming, even for a fast program like *grep*. I needed something better.

After a few false starts, I came up with the idea of indexing all of the mail messages. I wrote a shell script that did a *grep* on every file in the directories using all possible text strings. In effect, the index I created had "pre-grep'ed" the files. When I wanted to find a mail message, I looked in the index for a text string contained in the message, such as the author or the subject. The index would return a pointer to the file or files containing the string. This approach turned out to be far more efficient than running *grep* every time to find a message, although it uses a shell script.

This approach worked out so well that I passed the idea on to a coworker who implemented it on a much larger scale. Within a couple of months, he was using the same technique to index huge numbers of files on our systems. He refined the shell scripts until they could locate a string in several hundred megabytes of text in a few seconds—on our slowest machine. The application worked so well that most people did not believe that it was written in the Bourne shell.

While *grep* may be much faster than many commands run from a shell script, by using a different approach it is possible to produce a shell script with remarkably higher performance than *grep* alone. It's just a matter of looking at the problem from a new angle.

In this chapter we have explored the value of leverage. We have seen that leverage can be an especially powerful idea when applied to software. Like any form of compounding, software leverage produces extensive effects for small amounts of effort.

Each small program is a seed that becomes a mighty oak when sown.

Shell scripts remain an optimum choice for enhancing software leverage. They allow you to take the work of others and use it to your advantage. Even if you have never written a sort routine, you can have a sort routine written by an expert at your disposal. This kind of approach makes everyone a winner, even those who "cannot program their way out of a paper bag."

Albert Einstein once said "I have only seen two miracles in my life, nuclear fusion and *compound interest*." (Italics added.) For all of his wonderful theories, these two ideas impressed him most. Evidently he understood that a small amount of something, multiplied repeatedly, can grow to miraculous proportions. It took a keen mind like his to recognize the power in this simple idea.

On the other hand, maybe his wife used to sell Tupperware.

6

The Perils of
Interactive Programs

So Volkswagen was right. Small really is beautiful. Power rests not
with the big and strong, but with the small and capable. You only
have to witness the number of compact cars on the American
landscape today to realize that millions of people have arrived at
the same conclusion. Small is "in."

This fondness for the diminutive doesn't stop with cars
either. People are discovering that little things generally have
tremendous advantages over their larger counterparts. Paperback
books have long outsold their hardcover versions, partly because
they're less expensive and partly because they're easier to take
everywhere. Wristwatches have replaced pocket watches due to
their reduced size and greater portability. Technological advances
have given today's miniature electronic components more capability than much larger components in the past. Sales of pocket
TVs, palmtop computers, and handheld remote controls are sky-
rocketing. Even today's nuclear weapons are considerably smaller

than the ones dropped on Japan during World War II, yet they possess substantially more destructive power.

We owe much of this shrinking universe to superior technology. It takes highly advanced technology to reduce a mainframe computer to a microchip small enough to fit in one's hand. Without the miniaturization afforded by high-density microprocessors, many of today's products would be too cumbersome to be useful.

Still, it requires some level of user sophistication to be able to use these high-technology wonders. It seems as if the smaller and more advanced a device is, the more a user must know to be able to use it.

One example is the evolution of microwave ovens for the home. Early versions employed a start button and a plain knob for the timer. Then, as computer chip prices fell, it became chic to produce ovens that were programmable. These ovens were considerably more intelligent, but they also required more intelligent users to be able to take advantage of their advanced features.

Another way to look at it is that children don't learn how to write first with an ultrafine marker. They start with big, fat crayons. Why? Crayons require the child to simply hold on with whatever grip he can manage. Writing with a razor tip marker requires a greater level of manual dexterity. He doesn't acquire this until several years after he first picks up a crayon.

From these examples we can draw a couple of conclusions. First, small things don't interface well with people. While micro technology may be making things smaller, people aren't getting any smaller. Once a certain point of reduction is reached, people lose the ability to deal with things directly. They must resort to tools that enhance their normal senses. For instance, a watchmaker doesn't use the naked eye to scrutinize the tiny parts inside a fine Swiss watch. He must resort to magnifying lenses that allow him to see the components. Similarly, in today's semiconductor manufacturing facilities, microscopes are used to spot defects in integrated circuits packing hundreds of thousands of transistors per square inch.

The human senses function only within narrow limits. Sounds can be too soft or too loud to be heard. There are light waves at frequencies that surpass the normal range of vision. So, too, there are light waves at frequencies lower than the eye can perceive. With our sense of smell we can distinguish among perfume varieties or gag from the stench of a skunk.

As technology causes things to grow smaller, eventually they reach a point where our senses can no longer perceive them. Then a special interface is required for human beings to be able to deal with them. As computers become increasingly sophisticated, the gap between what exists and what the senses perceive begins to widen. The distance between the software carrying out a task and its user interface becomes an ever-widening void.

The second conclusion we can draw about small things is that, while they do not interface well with people, they tend to interface well with each other. Their small size gives them tremendous flexibility. They are readily suited for integration in many situations.

Consider this example: the next time you see a moving van in your neighborhood, watch how the workers load the customer's belongings. If they're putting an automobile on the van, it goes on first. Then they decide where the next largest pieces go. They follow these with the mid-sized pieces and then the small pieces. It's obvious. But what is really happening here is a demonstration that smaller things combine with each other in myriad ways to accomplish a task. While you have a fair amount of flexibility in the placement of the smaller pieces, the larger ones afford fewer placements.

What would happen if you had only small pieces? You would achieve maximum flexibility. This flexibility comes for a price, though. The more small pieces you have, the harder it is for people to deal with them. Managing them becomes a serious problem.

Similarly, in the world of computer software, having many small programs and modules gives you the greatest ability to adapt to the environment. Unfortunately, as the modules get smaller, the issue surfaces of interfacing with the user. The more modules there are, the greater the complexity in dealing with them.

This presents a dilemma for the software designer. He wants maximum flexibility for his application, so he constructs it from a collection of small modules. Yet he is also bound by the requirement that his software be easy to use. People have difficulty dealing with too many small modules.

UNIX takes a different approach to solving this conflict. Most other systems try to bridge the ever-widening gap between the user and the module performing the task with a piece of software known as a "captive" user interface. UNIX developers, on the other hand, recognize that this gap is ever widening. Instead of linking the user and the underlying modules via a mass of "spaghetti" code, they nibble at the gap in small chunks or layers.

Since we've just said that UNIX and other operating systems diverge on this point, you may suspect that there is an underlying rationale for this. The answer comes from the next tenet of the UNIX philosophy:

TENET 8
Avoid Captive User Interfaces

Before we begin a discussion about the reasons for avoiding captive user interfaces, we first need to define one. A captive user interface or "CUI" is a style of interaction with an application that exists outside the scope of the highest-level command interpreter present on the system. Once you invoke an application from the command interpreter, it is not possible to communicate with the command interpreter until the application exits. You are, in effect, held captive within the user interface of the application until you take actions that cause it to release you.

Let's clarify this with an example. Suppose you had two programs, one which lists the contents of your electronic mailbox and another which searches for text strings in files. If the mail and search programs used CUI's, your interaction might look something like this:

$ mail	Invoke the *mail* program from the command line.
MAIL> dir	Show the contents of the mailbox.
: :	
: :	
MAIL> exit	Exit the *mail* program. Return to command interpreter level.
$ search	Invoke the *search* program.
SEARCH> find jack *.txt	Perform the search.
SEARCH> exit	Exit the *search* program.
: :	
: :	
$	Again we're at the command interpreter level.

Notice the flow between levels here. First, invoking the *mail* command places you inside its own input interpreter. It forces you to interact with its command parser. The parser has a command set different from that of the command interpreter that called it. Second, to execute the *search* command, you must first leave the *mail* command by entering an *exit* command. You then call the *search* command from the main command interpreter. Once you're inside the *search* application, you must then interact with another command interpreter. This interpreter behaves differently than both the main command interpreter and the *mail* command's interpreter. The only similarity is that it requires you to enter an *exit* command to end it.

You can see that there are obvious disadvantages with this approach. You must become familiar with three different command interpreters, each with its own interaction "language." This may not sound too difficult on a small scale, but it can become prohibitive very quickly on a system having hundreds of applications. Also, while executing a command, you cannot do anything else until you exit from it. Suppose, for instance, that in responding to a letter in your mailbox, you needed to include some text from another file but you forget which one. You would have to exit from the *mail* command, do the search, and then return to the *mail* command. At that point you probably will have forgotten your context in the *mail* application.

So much for the obvious drawbacks. The reasons UNIX devotees eschew captive user interfaces are not so obvious. Before we explore these, however, let's contrast this CUI with a UNIX-style "noncaptive" interface:

sh> scan   The *scan* command lists the
                                contents of a mail folder.

                           :

                           :

sh> grep jack *.txt   The *grep* command searches for
                                the string "jack" in all files
                                having names ending in ".txt".

Notice that the UNIX user invokes all commands at the shell prompt or main command interpreter level. Each command completes its task, and control returns to the shell prompt. It is not necessary to exit from each command individually by typing "exit." The user need learn only one "language," that of the Bourne shell, a popular UNIX command interpreter.

The cynic might point out that the user still must learn the order of parameters to be supplied for each command invocation. This is true. But, with the CUI, the user must first recall which command to run, then which subcommand to invoke from the CUI. Therefore, there is nearly twice as much to remember. It is not surprising, then, that systems that employ CUI's often must provide highly developed "help" systems to guide users through the choices. On the other hand, most UNIX users get by quite well without complex help systems. UNIX commands often return simple messages listing the required parameters and their usage if the user enters an incorrect one.

Thus far we've defined captive user interfaces and touched upon some of their glaring deficiencies. The real reasons that UNIX users avoid captive user interfaces, though, run much deeper. They have to do with the way commands interact with each other. In the UNIX environment, no command exists in isolation. Commands interact with each other at various times. CUIs interfere with the ability of multiple commands to make this happen. Multiple command interaction is a key to UNIX.

CUIs assume that the user is human

Producers of CUIs base their designs on the premise that a person is sitting at the keyboard. They expect the person to enter responses to prompts provided by the application. The application then performs calculations or carries out various tasks.

The problem, however, is that even the fastest human being is slower than the average computer. The computer can conduct operations at lightning speed, and it doesn't get tired or take breaks. As stated earlier, people function only within a narrow range of activity. For example, even the speediest typists do not type much more than eighty words per minute. Most CUIs eventually reach a point where the user must respond to a prompt. Then even the fastest supercomputer is little more effective than the lowliest PC. Virtually all PCs capture text typed by users without the least bit of strain. As long as a system is constrained to operate within the limits imposed by human beings, it cannot function at its maximum potential.

I first became aware of this phenomenon when confronted with a window system running on a very fast workstation. Most people are accustomed to scanning text files on a terminal. Terminals usually allow you to stop and start the displayed output by pressing a <^S>/<^Q> combination or a "HOLD SCREEN" key. At normal speeds of 9600 bps or lower, most people control the rate of scrolling without any trouble. Today's window systems, however, have no artificial limit such as the communication speed to control the rate at which the system displays text. The user is entirely at the mercy of the CPU and its I/O capabilities. When left to its own devices, so to speak, the computer can display text considerably faster than anyone can deal with it by entering <^S>. This situation will worsen in the future as large cache memories and 1000-MIPS machines become common.

Because of the limitations we humans impose on computers, any system that must wait for user input can operate only as fast as the person sitting at the keyboard. In other words, not very fast at all.

Typical UNIX commands strive to perform their tasks entirely without human intervention. Most only prompt the user when they are about to take some potentially irreversible action such as "repairing" a file system by deleting files. As a result, UNIX commands always run at maximum speed. This is part of the reason a system designed for portability instead of efficiency still performs well. It recognizes that the weakest link, performancewise, in many man-machine interactions is not the machine.

CUI command parsers are often big and ugly to write

A parser reads the user's input and translates it into a form that the application software can understand. It has to react correctly to everything a user might conceivably (and inconceivably!) type. This causes the typical command parser to grow to gargantuan proportions. Sometimes the command parser will require more programming than the application's main task.

Look at this example. Suppose you had a program for formatting a hard disk. Since the potential for data loss is great, you might consider it "user friendly" to ask the user whether he really wants to wipe out everything on the disk:

```
FORMAT V1.0 Rev. A
About to format drive C: . . .
```

Formatting will destroy all files on the disk!
Begin format? <y I N>

The number of potential user responses to a prompt like this one is staggering. First, if the user wants to go ahead with the format, he may enter Y, y, Yes, YES or various combinations in between. Similarly, if he is sure that he doesn't want to proceed, he may enter N, n, no, or NO. These responses are fairly easy to parse.

The complexity begins when the user isn't quite sure what he wants to do. An unsophisticated user might enter "help" in the hope of getting more general information about formatting. A more experienced user could enter '?' to obtain a list of formatting options. Still other users might try to break out of the formatting command altogether by forcing it to exit by means of one or more interrupt characters. Some of these may cause the formatter application to exit ungracefully or even terminate the user's login session.

To handle such reactions, a command parser must be large and highly sophisticated, a "tunnel through solid rock" as described in Chapter Nine. You can imagine how large a parser would be if the application required multiple prompts. The amount of code would comprise the bulk of the application.

The UNIX programmer deals with the user interface by avoiding it, i.e., the typical UNIX application doesn't have a command parser. Instead, it expects its operating parameters to be entered on the command line when invoking the command. This eliminates most of the possibilities described above, especially the less graceful ones. For those commands that have many command line options—a cautionary sign to begin with—UNIX provides standard library routines for weeding out bad user input. This results in significantly smaller application programs.

CUIs tend to adopt a "big is beautiful" approach

Many CUIs employ menus to restrict the user to a limited set of choices. This sounds good in theory. But for some unknown reason, CUI designers are seldom satisfied with a simple menu having, say, five items. They usually add menu items that invoke "submenus" to expand the number of options. It's as if they're thinking, "Hey! I went to all this trouble to design this menu system, so I may as well use it for something." So "creeping featurism" takes precedence over brevity.

The marketing arm of the computer industry must also share some blame. The constant push for "features, Features, FEATURES!" forces software designers to expand the number of menu choices without regard to whether the features are truly helpful or even make sense at all. From a salesperson's point of view, it's not enough to make the application better. It must look better. If a program sells well with five menu choices, then one with six will sell even better. It doesn't matter that the additional complexity may alienate much of the target market.

There are technical reasons, too, for avoiding CUIs and their "big is beautiful" approach. As CUIs grow in complexity, they need ever-increasing amounts of system resources. Memory requirements explode upward. More disk space must be purchased. Network and I/O bandwidth becomes an issue. Consequently, computer hardware vendors love CUIs.

Programs having CUIs are hard to combine with other programs

One strength of UNIX is how its programs interact with each other so effectively. Programs with CUIs, because of their assumption that the user is human, do not interface well with other programs. Software designed for communicating with other software usually is much more flexible than software designed to communicate with people.

Do you remember the example of workers loading a moving van? We said that the large pieces did not fit well with each other and it was the small pieces that provided most of the flexibility. Similarly, programmers find it difficult to connect programs having CUIs to each other because of their size. CUIs tend to result in huge programs. Large programs, like large pieces of furniture, are not very portable. Movers don't say "hand me that piano" any more than programmers move complex, monolithic applications from one platform to another overnight.

CUI programs' inability to combine with other programs causes them to grow to massive proportions. Since the programmer cannot rely on interfacing easily with other programs on the system to obtain the required capabilities, he must build any new features into the program itself. This deadly spiral feeds on itself: The more features built into the CUI program, the larger it becomes. The larger it becomes, the greater the difficulty in interfacing it with other programs. As it gets harder to interface with other programs, the CUI program itself must incorporate more features.

CUIs do not scale well

CUIs tend to work well when dealing with only a few instances. By limiting choices, they can make it easier for an inexperienced user to accomplish complex tasks. As long as there are not too many instances, the user is usually content to respond to the prompts. The number of prompts can become unwieldy, however, when one must respond to several hundred of them.

A popular program (a shell script, really) provided by many UNIX system vendors is *adduser*. It allows the system administrator to add a new user account to the system via a "user friendly" CUI. Most of the time it works well. The problem with *adduser* becomes evident when you must add, say, several thousand users at once. Once a university had decided to change from another O/S to UNIX. Several thousand user accounts were to be transferred to the new system. It didn't take long for the system administrators to realize that running *adduser* that many times wasn't going to cut it. They ultimately settled on a solution that involved moving the user accounts file from the old system to the UNIX system. Then they wrote a shell script to convert it into a file resembling the UNIX password file. The irony of it was that the shell script to do the conversion was shorter than *adduser*.

Most important, CUIs do not take advantage of software leverage

Because CUI programs expect to communicate with a human being at some point, it is very difficult to incorporate them into shell scripts. It takes many lines in a shell script to carry on the kinds of dialogs that CUIs require. These dialogs can be so cumbersome to write in a shell script that programmers often resort to small user interface programs to conduct yes-no queries and obtain other responses from the user.

Since CUIs hinder interaction with other programs, they tend to be used only for their original purpose and not much else. Although you might suggest that may be simply "doing one thing well," it differs from small UNIX commands in that it exists as an application unto itself. It doesn't offer the same mix-and-match, plug-and-play features of its UNIX counterparts. It yields very little in terms of software leverage as a result.

Without software leverage, CUI programs cannot multiply their effects—and the effects of their developers—on the computer world. Although a CUI program may gain an early following because of its novelty when it is released, it soon loses its appeal as the rest of the software world marches on. Software advances appear daily on the computer scene, and a few ideas cause major upheaval in each decade. The monolithic CUI program is simply incapable of adapting in such a rapidly evolving environment.

Thus far in this chapter we have discussed how a captive user interface presents several obstacles to a piece of software's impact. Captive user interfaces make sense under certain circumstances, but they are the exception rather than the rule. Applications fare much better if they are made of a collection of small components that communicate well with each other. It doesn't matter much if they do not interact with human beings well. Ultimately this interaction is managed by a specialized program that, not surprisingly, is likely to be a CUI itself.

Programs that interact with each other are actually data filters. Each gathers several bytes on its input stream, applies a filtering algorithm to the data, and usually produces several bytes on its output stream. We say "usually produces" here because not all programs send data to their output stream. Depending on the data and the algorithms, some simply output nothing.

The fact that programs filter data is significant. All computers and their programs filter data. That's why we call them "data processors." To process data is to filter it.

If a program is a filter, then it ought to act like one, i.e., it should concentrate not on synthesizing data but rather on selectively passing on data that is presented to it. This is the essence of the next tenet of the UNIX philosophy:

TENET 9
Make Every Program a Filter

Every program written since the dawn of computing is a filter

Every program—no matter how simple or complex—accepts data in some form as its input and produces data in some form as its output. How the program filters the data presented to it depends on the algorithms contained therein.

Most people accept that programs such as text formatters and translators can be considered filters, but they have difficulty realizing that the same holds true for other programs not ordinarily regarded as filters. Take real-time data collection systems, for example. Typical ones sample analog-to-digital converters at periodic intervals to gather data for their input streams. They then select appropriate portions of this data and pass it to their output streams to user interfaces, other applications, or files for storage.

Do graphical user interfaces act as filters, too? Absolutely. GUIs normally process mouse button actions or keystrokes as "events." These events form the data stream fed to the input of applications on the screen under control of the window system.

The applications, as filters, respond to these events, effecting changes on the display.

There is also the question of those programs that fail because of hardware errors. Suppose a program encounters a hard error in reading from a disk. Instead of getting data back when it tries to perform a read operation, it receives an error status. Most of the time it will filter the error indication and produce an error message to warn the user. In other words, an error status as input produces an error message on the output. The algorithm that figures out the error message to produce acts as a filter for the error condition as input.

Programs do not create data—people do

People commonly believe that their applications create data when applications are really incapable of manufacturing data. Data synthesis requires creativity. It requires an original source of information. A computer has no original source of information.

When a person uses a word processor, the text being written comes from that person's mind. The word processor functions solely as a tool for gathering ideas and storing them in a format easily housed and manipulated by the computer. It cannot write anything any more than a hammer and a box of nails can build a house. The more intelligent word processors—the ones we call WYSIWYG or "What You See Is What You Get" types—may do some filtering such as formatting and justification, but they still do not formulate the ideas in the first place.

Real-time programs that gather information about the world around us do not create data either. The data already exist. By extracting readings from their environments, the programs perform a process of selection. Only important data pass through the programs' filters so they can be stored.

The world is full of data created by people. This data would still exist if the computer had never been invented. The computer simply makes it possible to gather and filter the data more efficiently. Any "new" data produced is not new at all. The computer just gives us an opportunity to manage it in a different way.

If the world were full of computers without any people, there would be no data.

Computers convert data from one form to another

An alternate view is that data, to be useful to most application programs, must be stored in a format that facilitates its manipulation. For example, the actions of a person depressing keys on the keyboard are of no value to a piece of software. However, once these actions are converted to a series of electronic impulses representing binary data, they suddenly take on new life within the machine. Then the software can convert it into a multitude of forms to serve any number of purposes.

An interesting side note here is that music is a kind of data. It has existed for centuries in one form or another. People have been playing stringed instruments for several thousand years. The piano, a stringed percussion instrument, has been around for many centuries. In recent years, though, the keyboard synthesizer has gained prominence on the music scene. The synthesizer is primarily a means to gather "data" created by musicians by moving their wrists and fingers. Once captured, the data can be filtered in limitless ways, resulting in the production of piano sounds and other noises beyond the capabilities of any natural acoustical instrument. In many ways, the keyboard synthesizer is in its infancy. Future synthesizers will bring us musical flights that will stretch the envelope of human audible perception. This will occur because of programs that can filter musical data in ways previously impossible.

THE UNIX ENVIRONMENT: USING PROGRAMS AS FILTERS

You may be wondering what it means for a program to "act as a filter." UNIX programmers follow a set of unwritten rules that simplify designing software that behaves in this manner. To help clarify these rules, I've included several guidelines here. Before we can discuss these, however, it is necessary to provide a short explanation of a concept in UNIX called *stdio*.

When a program is invoked under UNIX, it normally has three standard I/O channels open to it known as *stdin*, *stdout*, and *stderr*. Hence the name *stdio*. What is connected to the other ends of these I/O channels depends on how the program was invoked. In the default case, *stdin* collects user input when the program is invoked, and *stdout* sends any program output to the user's display screen. Any output sent to *stderr* also appears on the display screen, but this data is normally considered "out of band" or error information.

An interesting feature of UNIX *stdio* is that the devices connected to the I/O channels are not "hardwired" to the program. At the time of invocation, the user may specify that data will originate from or be sent to places other than the user's terminal. For example, *stdin* may come from a file, another program via a UNIX pipe, or even a satellite link to a system on the other side of the world. Similarly, if the user wanted to save *stdout* in a file for later perusal, he could direct the UNIX shell to place the output there. This provides for enormous flexibility with respect to the source and destination of the data.

How UNIX programmers deal with *stdio* has a significant impact on the ability of a program to function as a filter. If the program is written correctly, then all the adaptability of *stdio* can be used. Otherwise, the user is likely to be locked within a captive user interface. The key, then, is to write the software so that it employs *stdio*. Here are three important guidelines:

1. Use stdin for data input

Programs that obtain their input from *stdin* assume that their data could come from anywhere. Indeed it could. By avoiding "hardwiring" the input channel, you make it easy for the user to specify where the input will come from when invoking the program. Its source could be the keyboard, a file, another UNIX program, or even a captive user interface.

2. Use stdout for data output

As *stdin* usage allows your program to accept input data from anywhere, the use of *stdout* allows your program's output to be sent anywhere. "Anywhere" here may mean the user's terminal, a file, a printer, or even a digital speech synthesizer. The choice is up to the user, and it can be whatever is appropriate when the program is run.

3. Use stderr for out-of-band information

Error messages and other warnings should be sent to the user via *stderr*. They should never be part of the data stream sent to *stdout*. One reason for this is that the user may choose to capture error messages in a separate file or perhaps view them on the terminal immediately. Sending error messages on the same I/O channel as *stdout* can cause confusion further down the line. Remember that UNIX commands are seldom used alone.

Notice how this approach differs from that of other operating systems. Applications running on most other systems tend to hard-wire everything. They assume that there will always be a user sitting at the keyboard. They may ask the user if he would like to send output to a file, but they seldom offer him this choice unless a conscious effort was made to include this capability.

Hard-wiring the I/O implies that you know all possible uses for your program. This is sheer egotism. In an earlier chapter we stressed that everyone is on a learning curve. No one can predict how their software will always be used. The best you can do is make the interface to your programs flexible enough to deal with as many eventualities as exist today. Beyond that, let tomorrow take care of tomorrow.

After having spent many years in a software engineering environment, I once took a position in a telephone support center where I answered customer questions about software—in many cases my software. It was most enlightening to speak with customers who depended on the software to do their jobs. I listened intently to hundreds of them tell stories of how they were doing the unbelievable with my software. My most common reaction was "It wasn't meant to do that!"

You never know what people are going to do with your software. Never, ever assume that they will use it solely for the purpose you intended. You may think that you're writing a simple sort program, a word processor, or a file compression routine. You'll soon discover that someone is using the sort program to translate ASCII to EBCDIC, the word processor has become a public access bulletin board, and the file compression routine is being used to digitize *Gone with the Wind* for downloading over the local cable TV system.

It's easier to avoid developing programs with captive user interfaces if you keep in mind that all programs are filters. When you assume that the receptacle of a program's data flow might be another program instead of a human being, you eliminate those biases we all have in trying to make an application user friendly. You stop thinking in terms of menu choices and start looking at the possible places your data may eventually wind up. Try not to focus inward on what your program can do. Look instead at where your program may go. You'll then begin to see the much larger picture of which your program is a part.

When regarding programs as filters, software designers break their applications down into collections of smaller programs, each of which performs a function of the application. Not only do these small programs communicate well with each other, they lack most of the bloat required to make their user interfaces "bulletproof." In a sense, their "users" are other programs. These programs will ultimately yield higher performance. They are not constrained by human capabilities that will fall behind when faster architectures are introduced in the future. And programs, as we said before, don't complain, develop attitudes, or call in sick.

Now, if we could just get the programmers not to complain, develop attitudes, or call in sick!

7

More UNIX Philosophy:
Ten Lesser Tenets

Thus far we have explored the tenets that form the core of the UNIX philosophy. They are the bedrock upon which the UNIX world sits. No one could strongly contest them and rightfully consider oneself a "UNIX person." To do so would invite suspicion by the UNIX community that you lack commitment to UNIX and what it stands for.

Having pontificated on the dogmas of the UNIX "religion" we are ready to embark upon some of its doctrines. UNIX developers fight tooth and nail to preserve the integrity of the tenets we've covered up to this point. The precepts discussed here, on the other hand, fall in the "yeah, I kinda go along with that" category. Although not every UNIX person will agree with the points in this chapter, the UNIX community as a whole often aligns itself along these lines.

You will find that some items highlighted here are more concerned with how things should be done than why they should be done. I will try to provide some explanation for these, but be aware that some things are done for no other reason than that is the way it has always been done. Like established religion, UNIX has its traditions, too.

It is not surprising that proponents of other operating systems have adopted some of these lesser tenets as well. Good ideas tend to spread quickly in the computer world. Software developers on other systems have discovered UNIX concepts that have shown merit in situations where they may not have seemed appropriate initially. They have incorporated these into their designs, sometimes resulting in systems and applications with a UNIX flavor about them.

1. ALLOW THE USER TO TAILOR THE ENVIRONMENT

Many years ago I wrote *uwm*, a "window manager" or user interface for the X Window System. It provided the usual capabilities that many people take for granted in today's window systems: e.g., the ability to move windows, resize them, change their stacking order, and so on. Well accepted in the marketplace, it went on to become "the standard window manager for X Version 10." It holds a respectable place as the conceptual ancestor of popular window managers used with X11 today. The Motif Window Manager from the Open Software Foundation and *twm* from MIT, to name two, borrow heavily from the *uwm* naming scheme and startup file conventions.

One factor contributing to *uwm*'s success was an exclamation by Bob Scheifler during an early X Window System design meeting at MIT. Bob, a heavy contributor to the design of X, was reviewing my thin specification for the "UNIX Window Manager." Suddenly he blurted out, "Suppose I don't want the left mouse button to do that!" He went on to suggest that perhaps users might like to choose the function initiated by each mouse button.

Had I been a comic book character, you would have seen a light bulb suddenly appear over my head.

Uwm went on to break new ground in the area of "customizable" user interfaces. The X Window System made it possible for the user to choose a window manager; *uwm* took customization a step further by permitting the user to choose the behavior of the window manager itself. Combinations of mouse movement, button clicks, colors, fonts, and even menu options could be decided by the user. So powerful was this notion that the developers of X11 designed a "resource manager" that provided for user-level control of virtually every element of the display screen.

Earlier we said that the larger the investment a person has in something, the bigger the stake one has in its outcome. In observing how people used *uwm*, I found that if a person is given the opportunity to tailor his environment, he will. Built-in flexibility invites the user to make an investment in learning how to get the most out of an application. As one becomes more comfortable with the environment one has tailored, the more resistant one becomes to using environments where such customization is difficult or impossible.

Much of the UNIX environment revolves around this axiom. People generally find it troublesome to use UNIX at first because it is so flexible. The many choices overwhelm them. Eventually, though, they make an investment in learning how to take advantage of the many options. Once the investment reaches a certain level, it becomes very difficult to go back to other operating systems. They reach a point where their stake in UNIX has grown such that they would prefer to change what they don't like about it rather than leave it altogether.

Some people have criticized UNIX because, unlike systems like the Apple Macintosh, it forces users to make a significant investment in learning its user interface before they can become productive with it. With UNIX, they argue, it is too easy to shoot oneself in the foot. That may be true but, as colleague Jon Hall has asserted, it is better to let the user shoot himself in the foot than never let him run at all.

2. MAKE OPERATING SYSTEM KERNELS SMALL AND LIGHTWEIGHT

This one is a hot topic with UNIX purists and has been the subject of many debates over the years. The UNIX kernel consists of those routines that, among other things, manage its memory subsystems and interface with its peripheral devices. It seems like anytime someone wants higher application performance, the first thing they suggest is placing its runtime routines in the kernel. This reduces the number of context switches among running applications at the expense of making the kernel larger and incompatible with other UNIX kernels.

During an early stage of the X Window System's development, a strong disagreement arose over whether higher performance would result from embedding part of the X server in the UNIX kernel. (The X server is the part of the X Window System that captures user input from the mouse and keyboard and renders graphic objects on the screen.) The X server ran in user space, i.e., outside the kernel, making it relatively portable as window systems go.

The put-it-in-the-kernel camp advocated taking advantage of the smaller number of context switches between the kernel and user space to improve performance. The fact that the kernel was growing rapidly was of no consequence, they reasoned, since modern UNIX systems had much more available memory compared to earlier ones. Therefore there would still be plenty of memory left for the applications to run.

The user-space-for-everything crowd, on the other hand, argued that the X server would no longer be portable. Anyone modifying the X server would then need to be a UNIX kernel guru instead of a typical software application developer. To remain a competent UNIX kernel guru, one would have to forego much interest in the graphics aspects of the X server. Thus the X server would suffer.

How did the two camps resolve their differences? The system itself did it for them. After an apparently successful attempt to implant the X server in the kernel, testers discovered that a bug in the server would cause not only the window system to crash but the entire operating system as well. Since a system crash is considered even less desirable than an X server crash, most X server implementations today reside solely in user space. Chalk one up for the user-space-for-everything crowd.

By avoiding the temptation to put everything in the kernel, it is easier to keep the kernel small and lightweight. Small and lightweight kernels speed the activation of tasks in user space by reducing the number of data structures copied or modified when starting a task. This ultimately makes it easier for collections of small programs that "do one thing well" to operate efficiently. Fast activation of small unifunctional programs is critical to UNIX performance.

3. USE LOWER CASE AND KEEP IT SHORT

One thing people first notice about the UNIX system is that everything is done with lower case letters. Instead of operating with the <CAPS LOCK> key on all the time, UNIX users enter everything in lower case.

There are a couple of reasons for this. First, lower case letters are much easier on the eyes. If a person must work with text for an extended period, it soon becomes apparent that viewing lower case text is much more pleasant than eyeing upper case. Second, and perhaps more important, lower case letters use ascenders and descenders, the tiny lines that extend above or below the baseline of text, such as those found on the letters "t," "g," and "p." They transmit intelligible cues that your eyes pick up on when you read. They make reading easier.

Case is also significant on UNIX. For example, "MORE" and "more" do not represent the same file. UNIX employs lower case letters for frequently used commands and file names. Upper case is normally used to grab someone's attention. For example, naming a file "README" in a directory invites the user to read the contents of the file before proceeding. Also, file names in directories are usually sorted alphabetically by the *ls* command, with capitalized names appearing before lower case ones in a file list. This draws additional attention to the file.

While case sensitivity often causes much frustration for people who come to UNIX after having used a case-insensitive operating system for a long time, they eventually adapt to it. Many even learn to like it.

Another quirk about UNIX is that file names tend to be very short. Most frequently used command names are usually no more than two or three letters. Terseness is golden here, and you will find such cryptic names as *ls, mv, cp,* and so on. Very long multi-word command names are often abbreviated to just the first letters of the words. For example, "Parabolic anaerobic statistical table analyzer" reduces to simple "pasta."

The use of terse names is historical. UNIX was originally developed on systems that had teletypes instead of CRT terminals. Typing on teletypes was accompanied by bzzzt-clunk sounds whenever one struck a key, and a fast teletypist could do about fifteen to twenty words per minute. Hence, shorter names for things were quite the vogue. The fact that most computer programmers back then didn't know how to type had nothing to do with it. (Well, maybe a little.)

Why do UNIX users persist in using the shorter names today? Certainly today's keyboards and CRT terminals can handle much higher speeds, so such brevity is no longer necessary. The reason is that shorter names allow you to cram much more on a command line. Remember that UNIX shells have a pipe mechanism that allows you to string the output of one command into another on the command line.

This powerful feature is very popular with UNIX users. They often string so many commands together on a single line that, if longer names were used, they would exceed the standard eighty columns per line. One solution to the problem is to keep the lengths of individual commands short so more of them will fit within eighty columns.

A common misconception is that shorter names demand that people must spend a longer time learning the lingo of UNIX. The truth is, UNIX command names are no more cryptic than those on other systems. For example, most operating systems use the command *dir* as an abbreviation for *directory*, the command used to obtain the names of the files in a directory. UNIX uses the *ls* command instead of *dir*. While *ls* is as cryptic as *dir*, people mistakenly assume that UNIX is more difficult to learn when, in fact, *ls* and *dir* are equally obscure. It depends on the system you're first exposed to. Since UNIX is common at today's colleges and universities, many computer science students learn UNIX before other operating systems. To them, *ls* "feels right" and *dir* seems cryptic.

Finally, remember that what may be indecipherable to one person may be efficient to another. People in all walks of life use shortcuts to make their jobs easier. Abbreviations are common wherever information is stored and managed. Once people have learned them, they are no longer considered cryptic. So it is with the UNIX command set.

4. SAVE TREES

The term "UNIX guru" probably came about because UNIX is such an out-of-the-ordinary operating system. People who become experts in UNIX tend to be regarded with both awe and suspicion: awe because they have mastered the mysteries of this fascinating computing environment, and suspicion because you wonder if this person might be slightly off his rocker to have devoted so much time to what was once an obscure piece of software wizardry.

The first UNIX guru I met was my boss early in my career at a small high-tech firm in southern New Hampshire. Besides preventing many of us from playing *rogue* (a popular "dungeon" game) on company time, he also had responsibility for the daily management of our UNIX system. Our UNIX system ran on a Digital PDP-11/70, the same PDP-11/70 that had been running another operating system besides UNIX before he arrived.

In those days, much programming was done in assembly language. The engineers in our department would spend hours writing and testing code that would be cross-assembled to run on a target machine of a different architecture. "Bit-twiddling" of this sort required paper listings. Lots of them. To debug a program, a person would generate an assembler listing and send it to our fastest line printer where it would appear as a stack of fanfolded paper sometimes more than six inches thick. The more senior the programmer, the heftier the listing. If one wanted to gain respect in our shop, one simply had to generate longer listings. Obviously, anyone who could generate that much paper was certainly a hard worker, one worthy of significant compensation at salary review time. Management believed this myth, and we the engineers knew how to play it for all it was worth.

I was walking down the hall one day, laboring under a five-inch thick load of arboreal by-product, when my UNIX guru boss stopped me and asked what I was doing with so much paper. "This is my program," I replied. I practically shoved the listing in his face as if to say, "Yes, I'm hard at work. Yessir!"

He grimaced. "You're killing too many trees. Come to my office."

He went straight to his terminal and proceeded to give me a lesson on UNIX I'll never forget.

The point he made was this: once you have printed your data on paper, you have largely lost the ability to manipulate it any further. Data on paper cannot be sorted, moved, filtered, transformed, modified, or anything else as easily as it can on a computer. You cannot archive it in huge disk farms for instant retrieval. You cannot search it at the touch of a key. It cannot be encrypted to protect sensitive information.

Do you remember earlier when we said that data that doesn't move is dead data? Paper poses a similar problem for your data. It's simply not possible to move paper data as fast as electronic bits stored on a computer. Therefore, paper data will always be "stale" compared with data kept on a computer. Just ask the makers of popular encyclopedias of the past. They are having fits today trying to sell encyclopedias in lovely leather-bound hardcover book form when people can get more timely information from a CD-ROM or an on-line information service.

With the growing popularity of FAX machines, you may have observed that it is possible to transmit paper pages easily over telephone lines. But what happens to the information on the paper after transmission? It is locked into a medium that limits its usefulness.

Beware of paper. It is a death certificate for your data.

5. SILENCE IS GOLDEN

No, we're not saying that UNIX programmers shun multimedia. We're talking about so-called "user friendly" programs that overstate the obvious or treat the user like he or she is the software's best friend. Too many programmers believe that they're being helpful by addressing the user in a conversational tone. UNIX is unusually "dry" in that it provides "just the facts, ma'am," nothing more, nothing less.

Many UNIX commands ostensibly remain silent if they have received no input data or have no data to produce as output. This can be a bit disconcerting to the novice UNIX user. For example, on a typical non-UNIX system, the user might type the following command in a directory containing no files. Notice how the system responds by informing the user that no files were found:

```
$> DIR
DIRECTORY: NO FILES FOUND
$>
```

Contrast the above response with that of the UNIX *ls* command. When it doesn't find any files in a directory, it simply returns to the command prompt:

```
sh> ls
sh>
```

Many people familiar with non-UNIX systems often criticize UNIX for failing to inform the user that the directory is empty. UNIX advocates, on the other hand, argue that UNIX has indeed informed the user that no files were found by refusal of the *ls* command to print any file names. The lack of file names is proof itself that the directory is empty. It's like saying that it's dark in a room instead of saying that there are no lights on. A subtle difference, yes, but an important one.

Are there any advantages to having commands that operate silently when no data is present? For one thing, your screen contains only meaningful data instead of being cluttered with commentary that transmits little useful information. It is easier to find trickles of data if they are not surrounded by an ocean of detail.

Although this keeps things simple, there is a more technical reason. As we discussed earlier, most UNIX commands act as filters that are often combined using the UNIX pipe mechanism. For example:

ls -l | awk '{ print $4 }' | sort

The -l parameter instructs *ls* to produce a longer, comprehensive file listing. The pipe symbol '|' connects the *ls* command's output to the *awk* command's input. The {print $4} part directs *awk* to print only the fourth field of each line of text produced by *ls* and discard the rest. This field is passed to the *sort* command, which sorts each field in alphabetical order.

In the typical scenario, such as when the directory contains several files, everything works as described above. But what happens when the directory is empty? Since *ls* produces no output, the pipeline breaks immediately and no further processing by *awk* and *sort* occurs. If, however, *ls* produced "DIRECTORY: NO FILES FOUND" on its output to the pipeline, this would result in a strange "FOUND" message appearing as the final output from the *sort* command, since "FOUND" is the fourth field in the message. *Ls* may not seem very user friendly because it doesn't warn explicitly of an empty directory, but its design both informs the user that the directory is empty and makes it possible for *ls* to be used in pipelines.

Under UNIX it is important that you say what you mean. Nothing more, nothing less.

6. THINK PARALLEL

There is an old joke in the computer world that goes something like: if one woman can have a baby in nine months, does that mean that nine women can have a baby in one month? The obvious implication here is that certain tasks must be performed serially due to nature. No attempts to make the process run in parallel will make the result appear any faster.

Motherhood aside, there are many processes in the world today that can be and are done in parallel. Construction work crews, television production teams, and professional basketball teams are all examples of entities that must operate in parallel. To meet their goals, they function as a collection of serial operatives taking place simultaneously, each member of which fulfills a part of the total task. They meet at certain points to ensure their progress toward their goal not unlike the way semaphores and other interprocess mechanisms used in computer applications keep themselves synchronized.

In a UNIX sense, thinking parallel usually means that you try to keep the central processing unit busy. Most of today's CPUs far outdistance the ability of mass storage devices such as hard drives, floppy disks, and even memory chips to keep up with them. To get the most out of a system, you must keep the processor busy so that it doesn't have to wait for the peripherals to catch up.

The UNIX approach is to run multiple processes simultaneously, with each process scheduled to do part of the overall task. That way when any process becomes blocked while waiting for the peripheral devices, several other processes can still function. This results in enormous efficiencies. Consequently, UNIX often outperforms other operating systems on the same hardware platform in terms of the total work being done.

Parallelism also greatly affects how users perceive your application. UNIX users have long enjoyed "net news," a large collection of articles (files) distributed throughout the world via the Internet network and the UNIX-to-UNIX copy program *uucp*. The files cover an incredibly broad range of topics, and thousands of new files appear daily. Net news is the ultimate electronic town meeting.

One problem with net news is that some news groups, as they are called, will often occupy directories on a system containing thousands of files. Such directories are slow and cumbersome to open to obtain a list of files and their headers. Software in the past often required several minutes to open a single large news directory. This frustrated users immensely. It made it extremely difficult when one wanted to hop quickly from news group to news group.

Along came a program written by Larry Wall called *rn*. It reads news group directories the same as any other program with one small catch: it obtains directory listings "in the background" while the user is reading messages. It quietly does this action unbeknownst to the user. The key difference is when the user decides that he or she would like to switch to a different news group. *Rn* has likely already "pre-fetched" its contents and can immediately display them. It's like calling ahead for a pizza so it will be ready when you get there.

While thinking in parallel has obvious advantages for the *rn* user interface, it can have equally dramatic effects in other kinds of software as well. For example, UNIX allows a command to be run in the background by appending "&" to the command line. Commands invoked this way start a process running in parallel to the command interpreter or shell. It is possible to run several tasks simultaneously this way. This improves efficiency by keeping the CPU busy most of the time instead of idling while waiting for peripherals to complete their I/O requests.

A final point to keep in mind about thinking in parallel is this: no matter how fast a machine may be, you can always create a faster one by stringing several of them together. As the prices of

CPU chips continue to plummet, it will become more desirable in the future to run systems having hundreds, thousands, or even millions of processors. By devoting a small unifunctional program to each processor, it will be possible to accomplish tasks that most people consider impossible today. UNIX has already established itself as a leader in such environments.

7. THE SUM OF THE PARTS IS GREATER THAN THE WHOLE

The veritable claw hammer has been part of the carpenter's trade about as long as we have had nails. Used for both driving nails and pulling them, it combines two utility functions on a single wooden handle. Some claw hammers may have improved handles or tempered steel claws, but the basic idea is still the same. The idea has stood the test of time.

Or has it?

Most professional carpenters still use claw hammers today, but the hammer's turf is being challenged by new technologies. The hammer is no longer the best tool for the job, only a convenient substitute. For instance, nail guns have outpaced its ability to drive nails. They do the job much faster with greater accuracy. Nail guns enable workers to construct houses in a fraction of the time needed in the past. The hammer's claw end, however, remains secure. It appears that there is little that high tech can do for the universal wrecking bar.

Some people's software resembles the hammer. It provides a convenient conglomeration of functions that mate well to complete a task. The problem is, many integrated applications like these exist as large, monolithic programs. Sure, they get the job done, but they overwhelm the user—and the system—by incorporating features that may never be understood, let alone used, by the average user.

The UNIX approach to building integrated applications is to construct them out of a collection of small components. This way you load and use only the functions you need. You also retain the flexibility to modify selected portions of the application without requiring the replacement of the entire application. Consider the following figure:

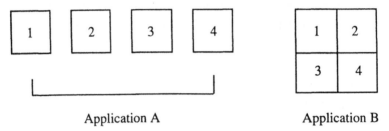

Application A   Application B

Both Applications A and B contain the same functions. In this respect, they are equivalent. They work equally well in situations where all four functions are required. Whereas Application B is a large singular program, though, Application A is a collection of smaller programs, each of which provides part of Application B's functions.

As long as you use all four application functions, there is little difference between the two. Let's suppose, however, that you wanted a new application that required only functions one and two. With Application B, you're stuck with all of B's overhead, even if you're using only half its functions. Application A, on the other hand, makes it easy to build the new application, since you need only "glue" portions one and two together.

Now let us suppose that you wanted an application that contained functions two, three, and five. Application A again makes it easy: you create a module having function five and discard functions one and four. Application B involves a more complex situtation that requires the software developer to perform "surgery" on Application B. This shouldn't be a problem, but monolithic programs usually don't lend themselves to easy modification. When a programmer builds a large, integrated application, he or she often compromises future expandability for the sake of higher performance. These compromises generally result in complex code that guarantees a steady source of migraines for the poor person who must make the modification.

Note, too, that Application B doesn't allow the use of pipes between its functions, while Application A probably relies heavily on them. This eliminates the necessity of having to relink the entire application whenever one function changes. This speeds up development and testing, since programmers who maintain Application A can work on smaller components that are much easier to manage.

One less obvious advantage of Application A is that it facilitates working in parallel by several developers. When programmers know that they are dealing with separate programs that must communicate with each other, they will place considerable emphasis on getting the interfaces between the modules right. This helps to eliminate lots of "spaghetti code."

You may be wondering how the user interacts with the components of Application A. One solution is for Application A to incorporate a separate user interface module. Since Application A's modules are designed to be interchangeable, it would then be possible to adapt the application for different kinds of users by changing its user interface module. The X Window System is a practical example of this. It enables the user to select a user interface from a wide range of choices in a "what you want is what you get" fashion.

8. LOOK FOR THE 90 PERCENT SOLUTION

When overnight delivery services like Federal Express first appeared on the American landscape, people marveled at their efficiency. Imagine a "pony express" that would get your package to someone across the country not in a month or a week but overnight. To many it was a dream come true. This service revolutionized the way we do business today.

The rapid ascent of Federal Express and other overnight delivery services raised a serious question: why couldn't the U.S. Postal Service provide this service? As we all know, the U.S. Postal Service can and does provide overnight delivery today. Still, many people believe that the commercial package delivery services do a better job. Why? It's because the commercial services implement the 90 percent solution.

Doing 90 percent of anything is always easier than doing 100 percent. In Federal Express's case, they do not provide the same level of service out in the hinterlands as they do for an area near a major city. Near major U.S. cities, it seems like Federal Express "mailboxes" are on nearly every other street corner. But try to find one in a remote town in the hills of Montana. It simply isn't profitable for Federal Express so it isn't done. The U.S. Postal Service, being a U.S. government organization, must provide equal service to all U.S. citizens. Therefore, you will find mailboxes on street corners in virtually every small town across the U.S.

By government fiat, the U.S. Postal Service must carry out the 100 percent solution. Meanwhile, operating as an independent carrier, Federal Express can focus on the highly profitable and much easier to optimize 90 percent solution. The result? Federal Express is very good at what it does. The U.S. Postal Service, for all its inefficiencies, does about as reasonable a job as one could expect from an organization that must do it all for everyone.

The 90 percent solution is one that results from deliberately ignoring those aspects of the problem that are costly, time-consuming, or difficult to implement. You can readily solve most problems in the world if you are given the opportunity to discard the toughest 10 percent portion of them.

When fast-track UNIX software developers design an application program, they strive for the solution that will give them the "biggest bang for their buck," so to speak. This means eliminating those functions that few people use and that are costly to implement. They ruthlessly cut such functions from the product requirements, often with an attitude of "if someone needs this capability badly enough, they can do it themselves."

Obviously there are some situations, such as heart transplants, where a 90 percent solution won't suffice. These are rare in the computer world, though. Remember that most software is a compromise in that it is never finished, only released. If, by definition, software can never be finished, therefore one can never develop software that offers a 100 percent implementation. By recognizing the 90 percent solution as a reasonable measure of completeness, it becomes easy to write applications that appeal to most of the user population.

That is part of the reason for UNIX's success. While it avoids trying to be everything to everyone, it meets the needs of most. The rest can write their own operating system.

9. WORSE IS BETTER

Anyone who has ever been in the military knows that there is the "right way," the "wrong way," and the "military way."

The "right way" is the way that I know is right, you know is right, and every normal person knows is right. It is what we consider correct—in every aspect. It is undeniably proper. The shoe fits. It works.

The "wrong way" stands as the inverse of the right way. Blatantly incorrect, it is wrong, dead wrong, no matter who looks at it. Your mother and father know it's wrong, your kid brother agrees, and your broker guarantees it.

The most enigmatic, the "military way" is by far the most interesting. While the right way and the wrong way coexist in an inverse relationship, the military way enshrouds itself in a cloud that is neither black nor white. It is the way in which those things that ought to work mysteriously fail, and—better yet—those things that should fail miserably unwittingly achieve unprecedented success.

The "UNIX way" is something akin to the military way. If you listen to the purists, it should have withered and died twenty years ago. Yet, here it is in all its parasitic splendor, feeding off the criticisms leveled at it by its critics and growing stronger every day.

Ingrained within the UNIX way is the paradoxical notion that "worse is better." Many claim that UNIX is not nearly as good as such-and-such system because its user interface is terrible or that UNIX is too simple to be considered a "serious" operating system. Clearly, if UNIX is worse than most other systems in so many ways, then it only proves that "worse" has better chances of survival than that which is either "right" or "wrong."

There exists a school of thought in the computer world that says that all "proper" designs should have four characteristics: simplicity, correctness, consistency, and completeness. It is said that designs should be simple, correct (bug free) in all observable aspects, consistent throughout, and complete in that they must cover all cases one can reasonably expect.

Most UNIX, programmers will agree that applications and systems should be simple, correct, consistent, and complete. The key is how they prioritize those characteristics. Although the "proper" system designer strives for completeness at the expense of simplicity, UNIX developers elevate simplicity to primary priority. So the "proper" system designer levels criticism at UNIX, not so much because it is "improper" but rather because it has its priorities reversed. In that sense, it is worse than the "proper" system.

UNIX aficionados, on the other hand, point to the survival characteristics of worse and say that worse is better. Look at the VHS videotape format, they say. VHS tapes are big and "clunky" compared to Sony's Beta tapes. They do not record nearly as well. They are hardly a match for optical disks. Yet, VHS tapes have clearly dominated the home video market. Similarly, the user interface on the IBM PC and compatibles comes nowhere near the practically flawless user interface found on the Apple Macintosh. Still, PCs are on more desks than Macintoshes, even if PCs are much worse than Macintoshes from a user perspective.

One reason for the success of UNIX is that it has always been regarded as an operating system that is worse than others in many respects. It was never used for any so-called serious work, such tasks usually being left to industrial-strength commercial operating systems. UNIX typically occupied the lower echelon of hardware configurations instead. It found a home on the mini-computer, a machine that lacked the brute force of a large main-frame but was powerful enough for more mundane work. Since minicomputers were typically used for less important tasks, it didn't make sense for hardware vendors to invest lots of money in minicomputer operating systems, at least as far as the scientific community was concerned. This tendency was further exaggerated when workstations came along. It became cheaper to simply port an existing system obtained for the cost of the media.

Some vendors and industry consortiums today are working to make UNIX better. In doing so, they hope that it will lose its worse-is-better character and finally be taken seriously. This could be a fatal mistake. For if UNIX is made into something that is truly better in all respects, then it runs the risk of extinction. In becoming "better," it will need to favor completeness at the expense of simplicity. Once that happens, UNIX will be UNIX no more. At that point, a new operating system would likely emerge that embodies the tenets of the UNIX philosophy better than the system UNIX itself may have evolved into.

10. THINK HIERARCHICALLY

The other day it became necessary for the first time to explain to my daughter how to organize files in a directory hierarchy. Before then, she had only a rudimentary knowledge of file system layouts. She understood that there was a directory on the family computer's hard disk with her name on it. If she clicked the mouse pointer on the correct icons in the graphical user interface, she could obtain a list of those files she considered her own.

Alas, youth has more time than experience. My nine-year-old had enough time to create a collection of drawings so large that the file listing would scroll off the screen. In the interest of making her directory more manageable for her, I showed her the benefits of creating multiple subdirectories for her picture files. It didn't take long before she realized that she could also create directories within directories, so she could organize her drawings in neatly organized electronic folders nested five levels deep.

She had learned to think hierarchically.

It's a simple idea, but like so much else in UNIX, it has profound significance. For while it seems obvious to many today that file systems should be laid out hierarchically, things weren't always that way. Early operating systems often placed system-related files in one directory and the users' files in directories all at the same level in the directory tree. People couldn't see the benefits of hierarchical thinking in those days.

Most modern operating systems organize files and directories in hierarchies, and UNIX is no exception. UNIX differs slightly from other systems, however, in the syntax one uses to reference files nested deep within multiple directory levels. UNIX is conveniently consistent in using the "/" character to separate the components of a file's path name. Thus:

/usr/a/users/gancarz/.profile

represents the file .profile in the directory gancarz. The directory gancarz is found within the directory users and so on up to the directory /, which is the "root" directory. The UNIX filesystem hierarchy is essentially an upside-down tree, with the root directory sitting atop successive branches (directories) and leaf nodes (files).

UNIX organizes other components hierarchically, too. For example, tasks in UNIX, known as processes, occupy a tree structure. Process No. 1, the init process, serves as the root of the tree. All other processes—including user sessions—are the offspring of init or its child processes. A process spawns a child process by creating a copy of itself and marking itself as the parent process of the child. Just as in real life, the child process inherits the attributes of its parent.

Another example of the hierarchical approach in UNIX is the X11 user interface toolkit found on workstations running the X Window System. It uses a resource manager that allows user interface objects, such as buttons and menus, to inherit attributes from other user interface objects hierarchically. This powerful idea makes it possible for users to customize fonts, colors, and other attributes in several components of an application.

Apart from the practical uses within UNIX, there is also a philosophical reason for hierarchical thinking. None could deny that most of nature is ordered hierarchically as well. To use an old cliché, the mighty oak that grows from a small acorn eventually will produce acorns of its own. Those acorns will in turn produce more oak trees. This cycle has been repeating itself since the dawn of time. Similarly, in human nature, parents beget children that in turn grow up to beget children of their own. The idea of a family tree has its roots, so to speak, in the trees of the forest. Since the hierarchical organization of UNIX mirrors nature, it's a very good sign that it's probably a good approach.

In this chapter we have explored ten lesser tenets of the UNIX philosophy. It is not expected that all members of the UNIX community at large will agree with everything discussed here. That is of little concern. UNIX, like the rest of the free world, allows for a great degree of individual expression and occasional disagreement.

Some of these ideas can also be found in other operating systems. Whether the UNIX community is the originator or the recipient of these tenets is unclear. Nevertheless, many UNIX users and programmers follow them, knowingly or otherwise.

8

Making UNIX Do One Thing Well

Most of what we've covered thus far has been abstract. Although we have seen that there are practical reasons behind every tenet of the UNIX philosophy, some of you may still believe that it wouldn't work in the real world. "Small is beautiful" is fine, but what about the big jobs? Is it really possible to build a complete application from a collection of small programs? Can a program without a captive user interface serve a useful purpose? These are fair questions, to be sure. Let's hope that you will find the answers to these and more in this chapter.

We're going to look at MH, a mail-handling application developed by the Rand Corporation. It consists of a series of programs which when combined give the user an enormous ability to manipulate electronic mail messages. A complex application, it shows that not only is it possible to build large applications from smaller components, but also that such designs are actually preferable.

Two programs—/bin/mail and Berkeley Mail—have been used almost exclusively for many years to process electronic mail under UNIX. Although Berkeley Mail is used heavily daily, both are poor examples of applications with respect to the UNIX philosophy. Both employ captive user interfaces, have limited capabilities as filters, and, in the case of Berkeley Mail, can hardly be considered small programs. Neither focuses on doing one thing well.

The MH mail handler, offered with many UNIX implementations, provides capabilities equivalent to those in both /bin/mail and Berkeley Mail. MH is a collection of small programs, each of which performs a function found in the other two mailers. MH also provides other small programs that perform actions not available with the other two, almost as if to underscore the ease with which one can incorporate new functions in an application modeled under the UNIX philosophy.

The following is a partial list of the commands contained within MH:

ali	list mail aliases
anno	annotate message
burst	explode digests into messages
comp	compose a message
dist	redistribute a message to additional addresses
folder	set/list current folder/message
folders	list all folders
forw	forward messages
inc	incorporate new mail
mark	mark messages
mhl	produce formatted listings of MH messages
mhmail	send or read mail
mhook	MH receive-mail hooks
mhpath	print full pathnames of MH messages and folders
msgchk	check for messages

msh	MH shell (and BBoard reader)
next	show the next message
packf	compress a folder into a single file
pick	select messages by content
prev	show the previous message
prompter	prompting editor front end
rcvstore	incorporate new mail asynchronously
refile	file messages in other folders
repl	reply to a message
rmf	remove folder
rmm	remove messages
scan	produce a one-line-per-message scan listing
send	send a message
show	show (list) messages
sortm	sort messages
vmh	visual front end to MH
whatnow	prompting front end for send
whom	report to whom a message would go

MH uses a collection of directories called folders to organize a user's mail. It stores each mail message as a separate file within a folder. The inbox folder has a special purpose: the contents of the user's system mailbox are first placed in the inbox by the *inc* command. Once mail has been moved to the inbox, it can then be selected and acted upon by the rest of the MH commands.

As you can see from the list, MH provides all of the capabilities you would expect from a comprehensive electronic mail application. The *scan* command displays the sender, date, and subject line of a range of messages in the current folder. The commands *show*, *next*, and *prev* show the contents of selected mail messages, the next message in the current folder, or the previous message in the folder, respectively. *Comp* and *repl* allow you to create a new mail message or reply to an existing one.

The major difference between MH and the other UNIX mailers is that you can invoke any of the mail-handling functions from the shell prompt level. This gives MH tremendous flexibility. Since each function is a command unto itself, you can call functions like any other command under UNIX.

The commands can be used within shell scripts and as filters. The output of *scan*, for example, can be "piped" into the UNIX *grep* text search command to quickly locate mail from a specific sender. If the folder contains so many messages that *scan*'s output scrolls off the screen, the output can be piped into the UNIX *more* command to allow the user to view the list a page at a time. If the user wanted to look at a listing of only the last five messages, "scan | tail -5" does the trick.*

The point here is that the user is not limited to the functional capabilities built into MH by the original programmer. One need only combine MH commands with other UNIX commands to create new and useful functions. This requires no new programming. The user mixes and matches the commands as desired. If the desired capability doesn't exist, it can be created immediately with very little effort. Many new functions are developed "on the fly" on the user's command line using this simple yet powerful architecture.

A valid question people sometimes raise about MH is, how do you remember which commands are available? Those who are familiar with the Berkeley Mail command, for example, know that they can always type "?" to get a list of available commands. MH really shines in this area. Since it doesn't use a captive user interface, you can refer to the on-line UNIX manual pages at any time. These manual pages are considerably more thorough than the short list of commands provided by Mail. MH's operation is therefore much better documented.

What about the user who prefers a captive user interface? MH provides one with the *msh* command for those users who enjoy being prompted for the next action to take. Obviously,

---

*These are not the only ways to do these functions. As in the rest of UNIX, many paths lead to the same conclusion. The examples shown were chosen for purposes of illustrating the flexibility of a UNIX-style architecture.

though, users are not locked into using *msh* if they choose not to. They are free to write their own user interface that works as a layer on top of the MH command set. For example, *xmh* is a user interface to MH that runs as a client under the X Window System. Buttons and menu items in the *xmh* application simply call underlying MH commands as appropriate. The *xmh* user interface presents a seamless interface to the user, however. It appears as if it were written as an application that performs the mail handling functions directly.

MH offers us an excellent example of a specific way to build a complex application under UNIX. The more general case can be illustrated by the following diagram:

USER INTERFACE LAYER

———————————————

APPLICATION LAYER

———————————————

COLLECTION OF SMALL
PROGRAMS LAYER

The CSP (Collection of Small Programs) Layer consists of a set of UNIX commands or shell scripts, each of which carries out one function of the application. As new capabilities are needed, it is an easy matter to create other small programs to provide the desired functions. On the other hand, if a more limited application is wanted, nothing must be done. The Application Layer simply refrains from calling those programs that are unnecessary.

The Application Layer decides which functions are essential to the user. The functions themselves are carried out by the CSP Layer. The Application Layer operates primarily as a "liaison" between the CSP Layer and the User Interface Layer. It also provides boundaries around the application. By unifying elements of the CSP Layer in a single environment, it helps establish the relationships among the small programs and provides the framework that ties them together.

The User Interface Layer is the part that the user sees on the screen when the application is invoked. It is highly malleable in that a variety of user interface styles can be used depending on the desired presentation. You'll find that three styles of user interfaces are common in the UNIX environment: the shell script or scrolling menu type, which can be used on virtually every terminal or teletype; the *curses*-based interface, a full-screen user interface intended for use with character cell terminals; and the graphical user interface, typically found on X Window System terminals and workstations.

A well-constructed Application Layer allows the user to choose from a variety of user interface styles, implying that the User Interface Layer should almost never be "hardwired." The user should be free to choose whatever user interface suits the particular circumstances. Thus a user can take advantage of the superior power afforded by a workstation when one is available, yet still choose to use a character cell terminal over a modem line in less accommodating situations. MH and its companion *xmh* provide an example of an application that incorporates this kind of flexibility.

THE UNIX PHILOSOPHY: PUTTING IT ALL TOGETHER

In the previous chapter we saw how the whole is often greater than the sum of its parts. This is especially true of the UNIX philosophy itself: each of its tenets hardly has the strength to stand on its own. Storing data in flat ASCII files doesn't buy much unless you have the tools to manipulate it. The goal of portability over efficiency seems shallow without shell scripts and the C language to accomplish it. Writing a collection of small programs makes little sense if they cannot be used as filters.

The UNIX philosophy is like a giant water slide at an amusement park. You cannot decide part way into the ride that you'd like to skip a few curves—you'll only wind up on the ground bruised and bleeding. As many have discovered the hard way, the UNIX philosophy doesn't work if you employ it piecemeal.

Embraced together, however, the tenets of the UNIX philosophy take on a broader, more powerful dimension. They interoperate and reinforce one another. Any criticism leveled at a lone tenet can be met by a response from another tenet. The old adage, "united we stand, divided we fall" rings true here.

Let's visit the UNIX philosophy tenets once more. This time, though, we will focus on the relationships among them, the goal being to expose the synergy you get by using them together.

Small programs have definite advantages. They are easier to understand because people have less difficulty dealing with a small "something" than a large "something." Being easier to understand also means that they are easier to maintain. Therefore, they are more cost effective in the end. They also use fewer system resources. This enables them to be loaded, run, and then released quickly, yielding greater efficiency, an attribute that must often be sacrificed for the sake of greater portability. Finally, small programs combine easily with other tools. By themselves, they do little. In concert with a suite of other small programs, they enable programmers and—most importantly—users to create new applications rapidly.

Small programs should remain focused, i.e., they should do one thing well. It is more important to solve one problem than a slew of them in a single program. By dividing large complex problems into smaller ones, it becomes possible to conquer them a bit at a time. Programs that do one thing well can be reused in other applications with much less difficulty. Their abilities are well defined and not clouded by useless "cruft" that can obscure a program's functional definition.

Small programs that do one thing well avoid becoming large complex monoliths. Such monoliths often contain "spaghetti code" and are difficult to join with other applications. Small programs acknowledge that there is a tomorrow where today's functional capabilities will appear incomplete or, worse yet, obsolete. Whereas monolithic programs cover all known circumstances, small programs freely admit that software evolves. Software is never finished; it is only released.

Because the world's software is in a constant state of evolution, everyone is on a learning curve. No one can predict with absolute certainty the directions that the software world will take tomorrow. The best that one can do is build software that meets the needs of today with the built-in assumption that it will change in the future. Therefore, instead of spending weeks or months writing design specifications, developers should document an overview of the direction they plan to take and then get on with it.

Building a prototype early is an important step. It helps the designer get an application into the hands of others early so that progress toward the Third System begins sooner instead of later. Prototypes accelerate the rate at which you move into the future. They encourage you to make changes at first when things are still fluid instead of waiting until everything is cast in stone. They show you what will work and, most important, what won't.

Building prototypes is much easier if you construct them gradually using small programs that do one thing well. They allow you to add functions as you go along with minimal effort.

Remember that software isn't really built, however, it's grown. As software grows, it will undoubtedly become more valuable as it is ported to new hardware platforms. New architectures come along frequently, and software that is portable can take advantage of them quickly. Therefore, when constructing prototypes, choose portability over efficiency. That which is portable survives. All else quickly becomes obsolete.

Portable data goes hand in hand with portable applications. Store data in flat ASCII files whenever possible. Again, we cannot predict the future, so you cannot know all the places your data might eventually go. Do not be concerned that portable data is not very efficient. New hardware platforms just around the bend will move your data around considerably faster than even the fastest machine can do it today. Remember, too, that the use of portable data also simplifies the process of getting to the Third System because the data is readable by humans at all stages of the process.

Portable software finds its way onto hardware platforms that you never dreamed of when you wrote it. In a sense, by writing portable software, you make a contribution to the wealth of software that has been written since the dawn of computing. Bear in mind that for whatever software you give to the world, you are also entitled to receive software as well. As your software travels, it will enhance the abilities of users to carry out their tasks.

The effects of nearly everything you do are compounded. Similarly, there are other programmers whose work is compounding. For you to take advantage of that leverage, shun the not-invented-here syndrome entirely. Create new applications. But do not waste time rewriting what someone else has already done for you. The software that exists in the world today represents a great store of wealth. As you sow seeds in that realm, be sure to harvest that which is ripe for the taking—legally, of course.

To greater enhance software leverage in both directions, employ shell scripts and other higher-level abstractions whenever possible. They take advantage of the work that others have done for you. Shell scripts help compound the effects of their work on the world, while enabling you to do more with less effort.

Shell scripts can be constructed much more easily if you have a collection of small programs to work with. Those programs won't be much good, though, if they require a user to type at them directly. Therefore, avoid captive user interfaces. Instead, think of all programs as filters. Programs do not create data, they only modify it. Make it easy for your programs to be used elsewhere.

9

UNIX and Other Operating System Philosophies

At this juncture, it is appropriate to engage in a short discussion of the philosophies of a few other operating systems besides UNIX. We're not going to delve deeply in this area, as we do not intend to embark upon a treatise on comparative operating system philosophies. But a brief foray into several other "religions" of the software world should prove enlightening, if only to illuminate why the UNIX approach is such a radical departure from other software design methodologies.

We will look at three operating systems in this chapter: the O/S of the Atari Home Computer, Microsoft's MS-DOS, and Digital Equipment Corporation's OpenVMS. Each has achieved success in its respective niche. Each has developed a following of loyal devotees. Each has characteristics that set it apart from UNIX, sometimes in striking ways.

If I manage to misinterpret the original intent of the operating system designers, I offer my apologies. As you might suspect, documented operating system philosophies are hard to come by. I can only hope that I have caught the essence of the designers' goals in some fashion. For our purposes, though, absolute accuracy is less important than the general thread of the design methodology. In that respect, the following discussions should serve us well.

THE ATARI HOME COMPUTER: HUMAN ENGINEERING AS ART

The Atari 800 and its less expensive sibling, the Atari 400, garnered a respectable share of the home computer market in the early 1980s. Primarily targeted as a machine for game enthusiasts, its major claim to fame was its advanced graphics and sound capabilities. Star Raiders, a Star Trek simulation incorporating stars and photon torpedoes whizzing by in 3-D hyperspace, propelled it to a strong position in the home market until it was overtaken by the popular IBM PC and the bargain-priced Commodore 64. Today its "player-missile" graphics (sprites) and display list processor are considered primitive.

Chris Crawford, a member of Atari's staff at the time, heavily influenced the design of the Atari Home Computer's operating system. His applications software (games, really) set the standard by which all later software for the machine was to be judged. Crawford documented much of his design philosophy in Appendix B of *De Re Atari, a guide to effective programming*.[*]

While the section's main focus was human engineering, it also sheds much light on Crawford's general approach to computing.

Crawford views the computer as an intelligent being lacking outward physical traits. Its thought processes are "direct, analyti-

---

[*] ©1982 Atari, Inc.

cal, and specific." He contrasted these with the thought patterns of human beings, which are "associative, integrated, and diffuse." The differences in these thought processes create a communication barrier between the human being and this smaller intelligence or "homunculus," as he calls it. The goal of the programmer, he believes, is not so much to make the homunculus more powerful as it is to break down the communication barrier between the homunculus and the person interacting with it.

This is where Crawford's approach and the UNIX philosophy part company. For although Crawford emphasizes that the most important thing a piece of software can do is communicate with a human being, the highest priority a UNIX program has is to communicate with another program. That the UNIX program must eventually interact with a human being is secondary.

In their approaches to user interface design, the Atari Home Computer and the UNIX operating system are galaxies apart. Most software for the Atari machine strives for "closure" or the narrowing of options. According to Crawford,

> The ideal program is like a tunnel bored through solid rock. There is but one path, the path leading to success. The user has no options but to succeed. [*]

To create the optimum Atari Home Computer program, then, you must limit choices. The user should be given only one way to perform a task, and that way should be obvious. There must be little opportunity for error, even if it means limiting choices. Flexibility and adaptability in the UNIX sense can only lead to chaos.

The Atari approach suggests that if the average person is given a gun, he is likely to shoot himself in the foot. By contrast, the UNIX system effectively hands the uninitiated user an assault rifle, plugs in twenty rounds, and points it at his foot.

As you might expect, the UNIX way can lead to havoc. Choices abound in the UNIX environment and limitations are

---

[*] *De Re Atari: a guide to effective programming*, ©1982 Atari, Inc.

few. There are nearly always a dozen ways to perform any task. This comparative abundance of freedom often pushes new users' patience to the edge of the precipice, as ill-chosen commands plunder their data and leave them wondering how to salvage it. But eventually most UNIX users find that understanding replaces chaos, and flexibility and adaptability find favor over artificial limitations.

Now, if we could just get Chris Crawford to write a version of Star Raiders for UNIX . . .

MS-DOS: OVER SEVENTY MILLION USERS CAN'T BE WRONG

MS-DOS, (Microsoft's Disk Operating System) is the operating system in widespread use on today's IBM PCs and PC compatibles. Over seventy million people use Microsoft's MS-DOS daily. If your measure of success is based on the size of the user base, then clearly MS-DOS takes honors as the most successful O/S in history. No other operating system can make that claim.

The "herd mentality" largely accounts for the overwhelming success of MS-DOS in America. While small cars opened America's wallets and bank accounts in the early 1980s, small computers captured the hearts and minds of millions of people who needed to store and manage information on a personal level, i.e., just about everybody. When IBM built a capable machine and used its marketing muscle to hype it to a public ripe for a "personal computer," the herd quickly adopted it. What better company to fuel such a revolution than the General Motors of the business machines industry?

So MS-DOS gained tremendous acceptance, not because it represented a giant step forward in the history of operating system development, but because it ran on a system considered a safe bet by the herd. Like the saying goes, no one was ever fired for buying IBM. Combine this with Microsoft's aggressive marketing of MS-DOS to PC "clone" manufacturers and you had a formula for a phenomenon.

Over time, this phenomenon began to take on a life of its own. As more people bought MS-DOS machines, software application vendors began to recognize it as the platform of choice. Additional MS-DOS software became available as a result, making MS-DOS more attractive to more people. This cycle continues today in a similar way with the introduction of Microsoft Windows.

MS-DOS does not have quite the same hold on the computer world in Europe as it does in the United States. One might attribute this to the fact that Europeans are largely independent thinkers. The typical European man or woman sits upon a rich national heritage that prides itself in its differences from its neighbors. The Germans will always be Germans, the Italians will always be Italians, and, *bien sûr*, the French will always be the French.

Because of the cultural diversities that exist there, the ratio of UNIX to MS-DOS systems is much higher in Europe. UNIX allows and even encourages multiple paths to software solutions, each of which may be valid given the right circumstances. This directly parallels the European approach to problem solving in the political and economic arenas, where common solutions often acknowlege the autonomy of individual nations. Similarities have surfaced in the UNIX world as it has attempted to rally around a common UNIX implementation. It is not surprising, then, that standards organizations in Europe have adopted UNIX as the operating system of choice.

So what is the philosophy behind MS-DOS? First, simplicity is paramount. If you're going to design an operating system for the herd, then you want it to be easy for most of the herd members to use. Hence, MS-DOS has a concise, limited command language. There is little latitude for the sophisticated user. On the other hand, the limitations of the command set are offset by an often verbose set of help and error messages. For example, the following notice is typical under MS-DOS:

```
WARNING! ALL DATA ON NON-REMOVABLE
DISK DRIVE C: WILL BE LOST... PROCEED
WITH FORMAT (Y/N)?
```

Second, by limiting user input and increasing system output, the MS-DOS designers have made the user more passenger than driver. This helps preserve the illusion that the user is seated at the console of a huge mainframe machine. Unfortunately, this defeats the purpose of using a personal computer.

UNIX has by comparison a fairly potent command language, so much so that even experienced users often fail to take full advantage of its power. Whereas the command language may be nearly unlimited, though, its error message set is painfully concise. "Do you know what you're doing?" is about as strong a warning message as you'll get from *mkfs*, a potentially destructive UNIX utility used to initialize new file systems.

Perhaps the most surprising aspect of the MS-DOS environment is that it incorporates some UNIX concepts already. For example, MS-DOS provides a "pipe" feature much like the UNIX pipe mechanism, as well as a treelike directory structure. MS-DOS also contains the *MORE* command, which functions similarly to the *more* command found in the Berkeley version of UNIX. This suggests that there may have been some persons familiar with UNIX involved in the early design stages of MS-DOS.

The UNIX pipe mechanism allows the output from one command to be fed directly into another command's input without the use of temporary files. A quick example:

```
du -a / | grep part
```

This "command" is really two commands, *du* and *grep*. The *du* command outputs a list of the names of all files on the system. The *grep* command selects only those file names containing the string "part." The pipe symbol "|" is the "pipeline" that allows the data to pass from the output of *du* to the input of *grep*.

Both the *du* and *grep* commands are invoked simultaneously in a style of computing known as "multitasking." As data becomes available on the output of *du*, it is passed directly to *grep.*

MS-DOS pipes differ from UNIX pipes, however, in that MS-DOS doesn't provide true multitasking capability. Only one command runs at a time, regardless of how commands are entered on the command line.

Future versions of MS-DOS, as well as Windows NT, Microsoft's newest operating system, are likely to contain additional UNIX-like features as the UNIX philosophy becomes more widespread. For example, MS-DOS Version 6 has added the ability to support multiple configurations of CONFIG.SYS and AUTOEXEC.BAT files, a move clearly intended to provide greater flexibility. UNIX has supported multiple configurations for years by allowing each user to specify a .profile file customized according to personal tastes. Windows NT has adopted much of the "portable" nature of UNIX in an attempt to capture greater market share by running on more hardware platforms.

Features providing enhanced flexibility and improved portability will probably be added at a rate just fast enough for the herd to assimilate them. Of course, at some point the herd may decide just to use UNIX.

OPENVMS: THE ANTITHESIS OF UNIX?

If MS-DOS is the king of the PC operating systems, Digital Equipment Corporation's OpenVMS is the king of minicomputer operating systems. Before UNIX had caught the world's attention, no single O/S in the minicomputer space had earned such a wide, loyal following.

OpenVMS owes much of its success to Digital's VAX line of computers, where the same software can run unmodified on a range of systems from the desktop machine to the large, air-cooled lab system. This compatibility at the binary level made it relatively easy to construct huge, fully integrated environments with a uniform style of interaction throughout.

Digital's approach to building systems is the envy of the industry. What Digital has done with OpenVMS and the VAX line has no equal in the computer world. Other companies, such as IBM and Hewlett Packard, have tried to unify their entire product lines around a single architecture but have failed. Sun Microsystems' attempt to unify the world around a single RISC (SPARC) architecture is an admission that Digital's idea of "one system, one architecture" represents a latent goal of all computer designers.

OpenVMS is a proprietary operating system. It was developed by a single company that is the owner of the software and any profits derived from it. Although written by Digital's OpenVMS Engineering Group in Nashua, New Hampshire, it really represents the aggregate thoughts on software that Digital's engineers have carried in their minds for years. The similarities to Digital's other operating systems are many. For example, users of RSX-11, an earlier Digital operating system, feel very much at home with the OpenVMS command interpreter.

The OpenVMS developers have strong ideas about what constitutes the OpenVMS philosophy. Like the developers of the Atari O/S, they assume the user should not only be amply shielded from any vagaries lurking within the system, the individual should be well-informed of their existence. If the Atari approach is to build a tunnel through solid rock, then the OpenVMS approach is to put lights in the tunnel.

Second, in the OpenVMS environment, if big is good, then bigger is better. This leads to the development of large, complex environments, such as Digital's All-In-1 office automation product, that integrate many closely related functions under a single user interface. OpenVMS has been quite successful in this area. The number of integrated environments available for specialized applications under OpenVMS would make even the most jaded MS-DOS user green with envy.

A third element of the OpenVMS philosophy is an artifact of the effect that the OpenVMS mind set has on Digital's customers.

Many people who purchase OpenVMS do so because they have a defined task to accomplish and are unaware or unsure of the kind of data processing required to provide a solution. While the typical UNIX customer says "I need this system" or "Give me that application," the typical OpenVMS customer asks "How can I do this with your system?" The difference may appear subtle, but it profoundly affects how OpenVMS engineers write software.

Applications developed by OpenVMS engineers tend to be feature rich. But the choice of features offered to the user is always limited to a handful of "interesting" options. UNIX application designers usually make no such presumptions about what is interesting. The choices on a typical UNIX system often include everything: good, bad, and that which may be safely ignored.

To a certain extent, an underlying belief of the OpenVMS philosophy is that users are afraid of computers. This might make you laugh if you've been using computers for a long time. The fact is, many people still feel threatened by computers. If they could, they would prefer to ignore the benefits of this exciting technology. Many wish that computers would simply go away.

Jon Hall, a longtime proponent of UNIX systems at Digital, has repeatedly asked a tough question: What about Mom and Pop? Mom and Pop, he would say, have a microwave oven but only use 59 percent of its capabilities. They don't trust any telephone that doesn't look like the wall phone in the kitchen. They have a CD player but don't know what quad oversampling is. They own a VCR and have yet to program it. In short, they refuse to learn about any technology that is not easy to use.

Mom and Pop—most UNIX advocates hate to admit this and yet readily do so—would have a terrible time with the "have it your way" approach of UNIX. Proponents of the OpenVMS philosophy dealt with this notion a long time ago. The OpenVMS developers are in the business of making the world's computers more accessible to those people who need bounded solutions, not do-it-yourself toolkits.

Besides the obvious user interface differences, there are other ways in which OpenVMS differs from UNIX. Because they are at opposite ends of the spectrum in so many respects, one could claim that OpenVMS is really the antithesis of UNIX. For example, OpenVMS usually provides a single path to a solution; UNIX often provides a dozen ways or more. OpenVMS tends toward large, monolithic programs with lots of options to accommodate the vast general user population; UNIX leans toward small programs, each of which performs a single function with a limited set of options. OpenVMS was originally written in assembly language highly tuned for the underlying hardware architecture; UNIX was written in the higher-level language C for porting to many CPU architectures.

A common mistake that people make concerning OpenVMS and UNIX is to assume that one is better than the other. The truth is, neither is better than the other. Each simply takes a different approach. In some situations the OpenVMS philosophy makes excellent sense, just as in others the UNIX philosophy is the correct choice. It all depends on who is in the driver's seat.

Just ask my mom and pop. Mom keeps a cup of water in the microwave oven whenever she's not using it to remind her to avoid running it while it's empty. She doesn't want cable TV because there would be too many channels to choose from. She wears an analog watch.

I remember the day Pop bought a VCR. He was so proud. He had purchased the latest in hi-fi, four-head video technology, "remote control and everything." I asked him to program it to record the David Letterman show Thursday night. His puzzled look and occasional snarls brought back memories of my first day on a UNIX system.

By now it should be evident that the UNIX philosophy is an approach to developing operating systems and software that constantly looks to the future. It assumes that the world is ever changing. We're not saying that we can predict the future. We can only acknowledge that, even if we know everything about the present, our knowledge is still incomplete.

Whether we are developing software or building a better world for our children, we see through a glass darkly. Someday we may know all the answers, but until we do, we must move forward, adapting to the future every day as it turns into the past.

The UNIX philosophy offers one approach, that of staying flexible. Storms may come and go, but the tree that sways with the wind survives.

Index

Printed and bound by CPI Group (UK) Ltd, Croydon, CR0 4YY

03/10/2024

01040437-0008